MODERN FILM SCRIPTS

D0889599

WEEKEND
and
WIND FROM THE EAST
two films by
Jean-Luc Godard
Simon and Schuster, New York

$2\frac{10}{5}$

Published by Simon and Schuster
Rockefeller Center, 630 Fifth Avenue
New York, New York 10020
First printing

General Editor: Sandra Wake

SBN 671-21279-6
Library of Congress Catalog Card Number: 72-76984

Manufactured in Great Britain by Villiers Publications Ltd,
London NW5

CONTENTS

A NOTE ON THIS EDITION

Since no full script exists for either *Weekend* or *Wind from the East*, the versions given in this volume are based in each case on a dialogue transcript combined with descriptive material obtained from a shot-by-shot viewing of the film. Technical description has been cut to a minimum to make for easier reading, but each change of shot is indicated by paragraphing for those who wish to make a closer analysis of the film. Nicholas Fry is responsible for the reconstruction of the text of *Weekend* and *Wind from the East*, the dialogues for which were translated respectively by Marianne Sinclair and Danielle Adkinson.

We should like to thank Connoisseur Films for providing a print of *Weekend*; Politkino for providing a print of *Wind from the East*. Our thanks to Anouchka Films, L'Avant-Scène du Cinéma and Politkino for providing still photographs.

Robin Wood's introduction to *Weekend* appeared in *The Films of Jean-Luc Godard* and is reproduced by kind permission of Robin Wood and November Books, the publishers. James Roy Macbean's introduction to *Wind from the East* appeared in a slightly longer version in Sight and Sound, Summer 1971, and is reproduced by kind permission of James Roy Macbean and Sight and Sound.

GODARD AND WEEKEND

by Robin Wood

Of the established major film-makers, only Godard has consistently, and indeed increasingly, sought directly to face contemporary reality. When an artist reaches the key position in contemporary culture that Godard now occupies, it becomes of particular importance to examine his work clear-headedly and critically and, if one cannot yet solve the problems the films raise, at least to keep them open and attempt to clarify them.

Total exposure to modern reality involves two dangers, neither of which Godard has entirely escaped. The first of these is the great formal crisis of modern art : the tendency of works that honestly reflect a fragmentary and disintegrated culture to become themselves fragmentary and disintegrated. The widespread facile acceptance of this among intellectuals has itself become a force of integration, but the problem exists, by whatever twists the advocates of the ' accidental ' and ' indeterminate ' try to evade it. The concept of a work of art which one can add to or subtract from at will is not new; it goes back at least to ' The Waste Land ', a work which for forty years now has consistently repelled all attempts to make sense of its structure. But only in the 'sixties has the problem become really acute.

The second danger of total exposure : the artist, sensitively aware beyond others through the very functioning of his creativity, may harden, perhaps destroy his finer sensibilities — the very qualities on which the fineness of his art depends — to evolve a protective covering of partial insentience. Godard himself is clearly aware of this : Paula Nelson, in one of the more communicative moments of *Made in USA*, wonders why she hasn't wanted to vomit since her involvement in the world of action (*'Toujours le sang, la peur, la politique, l'argent'*). In *A Bout de Souffle* Michel Poiccard protects and ultimately destroys himself by assuming the Bogart-gangster persona. Godard's own attitude was there ambiguous, and it has remained ambiguous ever since, through the embodiments of positive brutalism in his films — Lemmy Caution, Paula Nelson, the revolutionaries of *La Chinoise*, the hippy-guerillas of *Weekend* — and ambiguity can be a

5

means of subtly indulging tendencies the artist is rationally dubious about. Although the proposition that in the world we live in, effective action will necessarily be ruthless, and that to act effectively one must deliberately deaden one's sensitivity, is perfectly defensible, scruples about it cannot be dismissed as mere squeamishness; the question is whether one can sacrifice, for the sake of a hypothetical future, precisely those qualities that give life value yet which come to seem increasingly irrelevant. Perhaps the choice is between Godard and despair. One can nonetheless ask whether Godard's tendency to treat violence and horror as comic (the killings in *Pierrot le Fou* and *Alphaville*, the cannibalism in *Weekend*) isn't a form of cheating, or at least an aspect of the protective armour that is unacceptable.

The problem is extremely complex and delicate. Two factors must particularly be taken into account, both fundamental to Godard's genius : his habitual policy and practice of distanciation, and his determination to show only what is real. Paradoxically, the latter explains in part why certain things tend either to be not shown (copulation) or obtrusively stylised (death) in Godard's films. Godard as far as possible shows us things really happening, and happening in real places. But you can't yet show people actually copulating on the screen, and you can't have actors actually killed. So you either don't show it, or stick to your principle of showing only what is real : not a corpse, but an actor covered with red liquid (we are even allowed to watch one of the corpses in *Weekend* breathing). Godard's methods of communicating physical pain and death without actually showing the characters undergoing it are ingenious and interesting, in *Les Carabiniers* (where real death is introduced through newsreel clips), but even more in *Weekend*. What you *can* show is the real killing of a pig or a goose : the reality of the animals' blood and death-struggles is used as a stand-in for the human deaths, even more stylised than usual. Elsewhere in the film, the butchering of the heroine's mother is shown by pouring great washes of red liquid very unrealistically (they come indiscriminately from either side of the screen) over a skinned rabbit : the hideous and bloody carcass that *can* be shown is a substitute for the one that can't. One can, nonetheless, question the *adequacy* of such substitutions, and even ask whether there may not be some lack of human sensitivity in Godard that makes it possible for him to see them as adequate. Arthur Penn, after all, in the scenes of Buck Barrow's wounding and death in *Bonnie and Clyde*, made

6

human physical suffering real in a way for which the nervous twitchings of a decapitated goose seem meagre compensation. Such instances of vicarious horror apart, the stylisation is an essential contributory factor to the frequent semi-comic effect of the violence in Godard's films.

This determination to show only what is real is clearly an aspect of Godard's wider determination to expose himself completely to the age we live in, to make of his films an essentialised reflection of the age, and through them to bring his audiences to a wider and keener awareness. The function of the principle of distanciation in relation to this ambition is sufficiently clear. Its practice, though, may seem curiously contradictory, with its most obvious manifestation being the insistence that we are watching, not reality, but a film. The contradiction is more apparent than real : we are after all, watching actors before a camera, and in keeping us aware of this Godard is merely being true to himself. But his films are characterised above all by the continuous tension between the desire to show what is real and the desire to keep one aware of the film as film. The latter is Godard's way to complete freedom, with its attendant dangers; it also makes it possible to tamper with the audience's perceptions in a subtler and more insidious way, of which Godard may well be unaware. Our sense of film-as-film is a safeguard against taking things too literally; it can also become a safeguard — for director as well as audience — against taking things too seriously. Hence, when we see Lemmy Caution drive over a man's head, or watch a girl having a fish stuffed up her vagina in preparation for being butchered, cooked and eaten, it is our carefully fostered awareness of actors-in-a-film that makes it possible for Godard to present these things as half comic.

Humour plays a crucial role in Godard's distanciation, and it is impossible to draw any clear distinction between the legitimacy of this and the humour's brutalising tendency. There is not, I think, a single sequence in either of Godard's two most horrifying and desperate films (*Les Carabiniers* and *Weekend*) from which an element of comedy in some form is entirely absent. It is here that the private jokes, captions and doodles play their part. Again I find the effect ambiguous in the extreme. The comedy achieves the necessary distance between spectator and material, certainly (and also between director and material, allowing Godard to confront the insupportable with something like equanimity). At the same time it cannot but suggest a deliberate adoption of insentience (Eliot's ' Sweeney ' poems are closely analogous in this ambiguity of effect). Yet it also suggests an extraordinary resilience on Godard's part to the horrors (I am not thinking only of *physical* horrors) the films so uncompromisingly confront. Both films are characterised by an extreme tension between the utter blackness and despair implicit in their content and the alert, detached, ironic, humorous, exploratory manner. The overall effect of *Weekend* is not entirely negative or even depressing, though any account of its content would suggest it must be so. And this not because of any shirking or blurring of the issues : the final disintegration of civilisation as we know it is contemplated with absolute clarity and at the same time quite without complacency. It is as if Godard had unconditionally rejected despair as a useless emotion : however hopeless, one must go on enquiring. If Godard died and went to hell, he would immediately look around and begin making notes. This pervasive humour (at which we are only occasionally tempted to laugh) is usually quite distinct from true ' sick ' humour, which is essentially nihilistic and defeatist, inviting complicity in unhealthy attitudes. Even here, however, one is driven at once to make reservations : to judge the complexity of the issue involved, the reader might consider, as a test case, the question of why Godard made the butcher of *Weekend* a comic figure.

Distanciation in Godard needs further examination. One tends to treat as a purely artistic principle, as a matter of deliberate and impersonal choice, what is in fact organically related to Godard's fundamental attitudes and may well be a personal psychological necessity. And there is a consequent danger, with a director whose method is so objective and whose films remain so personal, that a completely individual and idiosyncratic view of modern existence, rooted in a personal psychology, may impose itself on audiences as objective truth. There is a perfect and revealing coherence in Godard's treatment of areas of life that might at first seem unconnected. In his treatment of personal relationships, especially those between men and women, one is struck by the fact that throughout Godard's films characters never make real contact and never help each other. Even in the early narrative films conversations between lovers tend to take the form of mutual interviewing, and the interview or monologue has become increasingly the standard form of communication in Godard's films. From *A Bout de Souffle,* which ends with Patricia Mancini betraying Michel to the police because she daren't commit herself to him, to

8

Weekend, which ends with the heroine eating portions of her late husband, relationships between men and women are invariably destructive (the only exception to this, *Alphaville,* is stylised and distanced as a fairy tale). At the same time there is an equally consistent sense of the need for complete personal commitment between people.

This ambivalence is very precisely reflected in Godard's treatment of social or political commitment. Though a positive interest in this is comparatively recent in Godard's work, we can trace a logical development from the earlier films. *Le Petit Soldat* was about a man trying to retract from political involvement. In *Pierrot le Fou* Pierrot's story on the beach about the man in the moon fleeing from both Russian and American indoctrination in order to run away with Anna Karina came across as an explicit rejection of commitment. The last moments of *Made in USA* in a sense repeat this, but give it a sudden positive orientation : the old alternatives of Right and Left are no longer a valid opposition, the questions must be posed in new terms, 'But what? ' — the film ends with a question-mark. Between *Pierrot* and *Made in USA* came *Masculin, Féminin,* which now appears the key to all Godard's subsequent work. It was the film in which the interview-cum-monologue (already used fairly 'straight' in *Vivre sa Vie, Une Femme Mariée,* etc.) decisively established itself as a formal device of crucial importance to Godard. Here, too, he began the direct questioning of immediate environmental reality, and hence the forcing of the spectator into direct confrontation with it, that is developed through *Deux ou Trois Choses* and *La Chinoise* to certain sections of *Weekend* (the monologues of the Algerian and black African garbage collectors). It is in *Masculin, Féminin* also that Godard's *positive* interest in the possibilities of political action first appears, to become of central importance in the subsequent films. When Godard made *La Chinoise,* a rumour circulated widely over here that he had suddenly become committed to the tenets of Maoist Communism. As this film (and its two immediate predecessors) has still not received a public screening in this country outside the NFT, it is perhaps worth insisting that there is no cinematic evidence of this. What *La Chinoise* reveals is an intense interest, in the spirit of positive enquiry, in the involvement with Maoist Communism of young French intellectuals. The films from *Masculin, Féminin* onwards are increasingly full of direct statements to the audience, but none of these can be shown to come from Godard himself : they are simply pieces of evidence, testimonies, frequently contradicted or counterbalanced by others within the same film. What is clear is that Godard's desire for positive commitment has increased greatly in his recent films, and the films are characterised by the perpetual tension between this intense desire and a correspondingly intense distrust. Stylistically this basic characteristic of Godard is expressed in the tension between the urge to confront actuality head-on and the all-pervading distanciation, which perfectly expresses this holding-back from commitment. Both Godard's peculiar genius, that makes him the most important contemporary film-maker, and the limitations that are inseparable from it, are determined by this characteristic. No other director in my experience makes one so acutely aware of what life today entails; at the same time, most of us have experienced considerable exasperation at the tendency of Godard's films — especially the freer ones — to say a little about everything and not very much about anything. The exasperation is a superficial response to one of the more superficial aspects of Godard's work — a Godard film is always more than the sum of its reference — but it is not entirely without justification.

Godard's work reveals, in somewhat uneasy relationship to each other, both revolutionary and traditionalist tendencies. The former has always been the more obvious, expressing itself in style and method. Traditional in character, however, is the importance attached to the need (though always frustrated) for final personal commitment between man and woman. There is also the obsessive outpouring of cultural references in the films, as if, having rejected the traditions on which modern society is built, Godard were trying to build up a tradition of his own, by selecting from the European (and American) cultural tradition as a whole (a process paralleled in the work of Eliot, Stravinsky and Picasso). Godard has always, I think, suspected the validity of this : he has been too acutely aware of the gulf between the arts and the greater part of active human existence. The attempt to fuse this personal tradition with dynamic action, by equipping Lemmy Caution with Eluard, now looks like desperate cheating. The revolutionary side of Godard has always been the stronger, and its dominance has increased decisively in the films from *Masculin, Féminin* on. As one might expect, the cultural references have tended to diminish in direct ratio to the development of Godard's interest in political action. The *action musicale* sequence (or rather shot — it consists of a single long take) in *Weekend* is of particular significance here. On

10

one level the scene is a joke about Malraux's policy of bringing culture to the people (the caption itself contains a play on the word *' action '*, in the cinematic and political senses) : the Mozart piano sonata performed on a grand piano in a farmyard to an audience mostly of tractors, incurious labourers and impassive peasant women. But it is also Godard's personal farewell to the European cultural tradition. The scene is given an ironic formal elegance and symmetry corresponding to form in classical music. The take consists of the camera circling the farmyard three times, twice in one direction, the third time in the reverse. The first two circuits are timed to correspond exactly with the pianist's two playings of the first movement exposition; during the third the classical symmetry is confirmed by having the labourer whose exit towards a barn was followed in the first camera circuit, exactly reverse the movement, paralleling the reversed camera-track. Thus Godard isolates the scene formally from the rest of the film. The thrice-repeated circuit of the farmyard conveys a sense of enclosure, insisting on the total irrelevance of the Mozart performance — and the Mozartian sensibility — to the world of pile-ups and general disintegration outside. The pianist's enthusiastic dissertations on the music recall very strikingly the Shakespeare lesson in *Bande à Part:* here, the sense of incongruity and dislocation is even more extreme. (It is interesting that both Godard and Bergman, at almost the same time, should have used Mozart to stress, in the words of Max von Sydow, the ' utter unimportance of art in the world of men ').

In *Viridiana,* too, Mozart and Handel gave place to raucous pop music (' Shake your cares away '); in *Weekend* Mozart gives place to the hippy-guerrillas' drum improvisations. The spirit could scarcely be more different. Buñuel gives us quite simply the end; there is no sense of any possible sequel or recommencement. What makes *Weekend* so much more insupportable is Godard's refusal to see the end of civilisation as final. It is insidiously flattering to the liberal-humanist ego to be able to equate the end of western civilisation with the end of the world. But *Weekend* is not about the end of the world — it is simply about the end of *our* world. Just to dare to imagine *Weekend* is an act of heroism of a kind only possible to an artist who has achieved an exceptional degree of personal freedom. The film postulates, rather convincingly, the irrelevance, uselessness, and ultimate disintegration of everything I have always believed in, worked for, and found worth

11

living for, and I don't think I can be unique or even unusual in this. Hence my difficulty in tolerating the rather complacent, only *half-shocked* amusement with which many people receive it. (Yet Godard is partly responsible for this : jokes of the ' Arizona Jules ' variety may be necessary if the film is to be supportable at all, yet at the same time they encourage a response of complacent spot-the-allusion smartness). *Weekend* must be taken very seriously indeed, its implications and attitudes subjected to the most rigorous scrutiny.

Weekend pushes to logical extremes just about everything present in Godard's previous work. All his feelings about capitalist society (whose representatives in earlier films range from the party guests in *Pierrot le Fou* to the inhabitants of the wasteland of *Les Carabiniers*) reach definitive expression in his depiction of the relationships and values of the characters of *Weekend*. Offered the fulfilment of their desires, the ' educated ' bourgeois couple, like the semi-literates of *Les Carabiniers,* can think only of the basely material — hotels at Miami Beach and weekends with James Bond. Sexual experience, driven for kicks to the weirdest perversions, has become a matter of farcical inanity and discomfort. Relationships resemble a grotesque parody of those in earlier Godard films : each partner has been trying for some time to murder the other; as the wife is raped in a ditch by a passing tramp, not only does the husband (who refused the tramp a light for his cigarette) show not the slightest indignation or interest — it doesn't even occur to the wife to rebuke him afterwards. At the end of the film she enjoys eating him, not in any spirit of symbolic possessiveness but simply as a tasty bit of meat. Godard shows us a world that is disintegrating primarily from its own perverted viciousness and debasement. This is acceptable as a savagely caricatured depiction of the essential nature of materialistic society; yet it is worth remembering — naive as this may sound — that that society consists of millions of human beings, corrupted doubtless by materialism to a greater or lesser degree, but that ' greater or lesser ' allows for a wide range of human possibilities. The simplification makes it that much easier for Godard to accept the necessity for (as well as the inevitability of) total ruthlessness.

Godard uses the ' Third World ' monologues of the Algerian and the black African as a focal point for the film, punctuating them with flash-backs to earlier scenes (but generally using either alternative takes or continuations not shown before) and one flash-forward to the guerrillas. The monologues stress the necessity for violence and ruthlessness among the emergent peoples, and the formal device relates this to all the other parts of the film, giving it a more generalised significance, placing it in the context of western civilisation and its disintegration. The hippy-guerrilla-cannibals emerge as at once the logical outcome of what has gone before, and the possibility of a new beginning. The latter is present in the film only tentatively : it is difficult to feel the guerrillas as other than completely negative, but not quite impossible. They represent the kind of reaction the society we have been shown *must* produce : dehumanised (from the viewpoint of any civilised concept of humanity), brutish, almost devoid of any generous, outgoing feelings towards other human beings (a characteristic they share with virtually all Godard's characters). In the scene in which they are introduced, they massacre a party of bourgeois picnickers, including presumably a child (we just see the machine-gunning, with the victims off-screen, which could be seen as distanciation or simply cheating, depending on how sympathetic one is feeling towards Godard). The recurrent image of one or other of the guerrillas improvising in solitary self-absorption on a percussion battery seems central to the presentation : percussion (of such wide significance in the development of contemporary music) has itself a dehumanised quality, representing a stripping away of all *emotional* sensitivity to a purely nervous-physical level of experience. The cannibalistic ' rites ' (if that is what they are) with eggs and live fish are a fulfilment of the heroine's fantasy (if that is what it was) at the start of the film; but deprived even of the debased eroticism that was its *raison d'être*. Nor is this replaced — as some have suggested — by a sense of tribal ritual : the action is presented as entirely arbitrary and meaningless, without the least communal significance. (It is difficult to feel sure to what degree the disgust the scene in question evokes is occasioned by its actual content and to what degree by our sense that Godard finds it amusing.) There is absolutely no sense of any constructive aim or programme.

But if the guerrillas seem in most obvious ways an end rather than a beginning, there is nevertheless a strong sense that something new might grow out of them; yet it would be something that left out of account virtually everything most of us value in the civilised tradition, in terms of sensibility as well as of achievement. The guerrillas supply the film's one moment of transitory tenderness, in the moment after the gun-battle when a girl dies singing, in a young man's arms. He goes off at once with another girl. But even the meagre fact that he props her up until she is dead counts for something in the context of human behaviour depicted in the rest of the film; and the spirit behind the apparent callousness is quite different — given the precariousness of their existence, the guerrillas are living by the code they have to live by. Their position is founded on a terrible honesty, quite without illusions or ideals, an acceptance of man's innate bestiality. There is a clear contrast between the recitation over drum music by the lake and the diatribe of Saint-Just in the meadows; the impassioned protest of the earlier speech gives place to an acceptance of the horror of man, and it is on precisely this note that the film ends : the guerrilla talking about the bottomless appallingness of human nature as he and the heroine pick at a mélange of pork, English tourist, and bits of her husband. Hence the end-caption, ' *Fin de Cinéma* ' (for ' *Cinéma* ' read ' *the Arts* '): if the future *Weekend* postulates, with its disturbing balance of horror and hopefulness, comes about, it will entail the final destruction of all those finer human feelings that the European cultural tradition (in *Weekend*, Mozart) embodies.

I think one can draw a revealing comparison between *Weekend* and another great film about social disintegration, *The Chase*. Penn's film, it will be seen at once, has all those human qualities that Godard's lacks : a sense of the possibility of mature, adult relationship (Brando and Angie Dickinson), and of the possibility of tenderness and warmth of sympathetic response between people (Jane Fonda — Robert Redford — James Fox), and an ability to see human beings, even large contemptible ones, in the round, with a certain generosity. Yet it is possession of these qualities that makes it impossible for him to present other than a tragic and despairing view of life, whereas it is precisely Godard's lack of them that enables him to go beyond this. It makes *Weekend* the most frightening, exciting and challenging film I have ever seen : the challenge lying in its horrifying optimism.

14

CREDITS:

Script by	Jean-Luc Godard
Directed by	Jean-Luc Godard
Production company	Comacico/Les Films Copernic/Lira Films (Paris)/Ascot Cineraid (Rome)
Director of photography	Raoul Coutard
Music	Antoine Duhamel; Mozart's piano sonata K 576
Song ' Allo, tu m'entends '	Guy Béart
Assistant director	Claude Miler
Production manager	Ralph Baum, Philippe Senné
Editor	Agnes Guillemot
Sound	René Levert
Made in location in	Paris region, September-October 1967
Colour process	Eastman Colour
Length	8,550 feet
Running time	95 minutes
First shown	Paris, 29 December 1967

CAST:

Mireille Darc	Corinne
Jean Yanne	Roland
Jean-Pierre Kalfon	Leader of the FLSO
Valérie Lagrange	His Moll
Jean-Pierre Léaud	Saint-Just/Young Man in the phone booth
Yves Beneyton	Member of the FLSO
Paul Gégauff	Pianist
Daniel Pommereulle	Joseph Balsamo
Yves Afonso	Tom Thumb
Blandine Jeanson	Emily Brontë/Girl in farmyard
Ernest Menzer	Cook
Georges Staquet	Tractor Driver
Juliet Berto	Girl in car crash/Member of the FLSO
Anna Wiazemsky	Girl in farmyard/Member of the FLSO
Virginie Vignon	Marie Madeleine
Monsieur Jojot	
Isabelle Pons	

15

WEEKEND

TITLE blue letters :   LES FILMS
                        COPERNIC
                        PRESENT

TITLE blue letters :   A FILM
                        ADRIFT
                        IN THE
                        COSMOS

We hear the roar of traffic and a murmur of conversation. A phone rings then a woman's voice speaks.

CORINNE off : *It's for you.*

The title cuts and we find ourselves in the penthouse of a Paris apartment block, looking out through some french windows to a terrace with green trees beyond. Two men, ROLAND and a FRIEND, are seated outside, chatting, a table laden with drinks in front of them.

ROLAND getting up : *Who is it?*

He comes in through the french windows and goes off to answer the telephone.

CORINNE off : *The office . . . Afterwards, could you ring Mother to find out if it's all right about the clinic?*

ROLAND off : *I told you, I've already done it.*

CORINNE appears just in front of camera, speaking over her shoulder to ROLAND.

CORINNE : *I guess she didn't understand. She's expecting us after lunch.*

She stands on the threshold and snaps her fingers at the FRIEND out on the terrace, then comes back into the apartment and goes off in the direction she appeared from. Camera pans, following the FRIEND from inside the glass-walled apartment as he walks round to another part of the terrace and sits down on a stone bench. In the background, CORINNE is standing looking down into the street below, seen between a couple of potted cypress trees.

FRIEND : *Wouldn't it be great when Roland drives your father home*

17

if both of them died in an accident?

He holds out Corinne's drink. She comes and takes it from him.

Title blue letters :   A FILM FOUND
        ON A SCRAP-HEAP

Resume on the two of them in medium close-up as Corinne takes her drink from the Friend. She is slim, sexy, very Parisian, with short blonde hair and a pouting face.

Friend : *Did he get his brakes mended?*

Camera pans with Corinne as she walks to the edge of the terrace again and looks down.

Corinne over her shoulder : *No. I managed to make him forget . . .*

Friend off : *Did you know that seven people got killed last Sunday at the Evreux junction?*

She turns and leans back against the balcony rail, fiddling with her glass.

Corinne : *Yeah, that would be great . . .*

There is loud hooting in the street below. She half turns and looks down again.

Title red, white and blue letters :
        END WEEK END
        WEEK END WEE
        K END WEEK EN
        D WEEK END WE
        EK END WEEK E
        ND WEEK END W
        EEK END WEEK

A high shot of the street below as seen by Corinne. A red Matra coupé has collided with a blue and white Mini. There is furious hooting as it backs off and tries to drive away; but the Mini driver leaps in front of it, tears open the driver's door and starts a fight. The red car's passenger jumps out also and runs round the front of it to join in.

Resume on Corinne from a low angle, three-quarter back view, looking down into the street; there is more furious hooting and shouting. The Friend stands just behind her with his hand on her arm.

Friend ruffling her hair : *But what'll you do?* He goes off.

18

CORINNE turning towards him : *I'm not driving back with them, I can tell you that. I'll make up some story about having bronchitis.* She looks down into the street again, then back at the FRIEND. *What are you thinking?*

FRIEND off : *Don't you think Roland's getting suspicious? Sometimes he looks at me in a funny sort of way.*

CORINNE shrugging : *No he isn't. You know, I have to let him screw me from time to time so he thinks I love him.* She turns back to the scene below.

> Down in the street, the three men are still fighting furiously, chasing one another around the two cars. The red car's driver swipes at the Mini driver with a belt, while his passenger gets a pile of groceries from inside the Mini and starts pelting the driver with them. Finally the latter is brought to the ground beside his own vehicle and the red car's driver starts punching him viciously. The passenger hops around in anxiety while his colleague puts in a few kicks to the kidneys for good measure, then they leap into their car and speed away . . . Theme music in. The Mini driver gets painfully to his feet, holding his head.

> ROLAND comes into the bedroom of the apartment from another part of the terrace, having obviously been watching the fight too. He is dark and heavy-featured; there is something brutal about all his movements and a cigarette hangs perpetually from his lips. Camera tilts down with him as he sits on the bed and picks up the telephone.

ROLAND : *Listen, you're not to phone me here any more; it's dangerous . . . Yeah, it was a guy who was hitting another who'd bumped into his headlamp . . . for a moment I really thought he was dead. . . . Yeah, wouldn't it be great if it had been her . . . No, first the money . . . Listen, if I always say that it's because I love you . . . uh . . . I've got to be cautious after those sleeping pills and the gas . . . She may be dumb but she'll start getting suspicious in the end. Anyway, the main thing is for her old man to croak. Afterwards, when Corinne's got the money, we'll deal with her . . . Of course I love you . . . You're a great big lovely bitch and you know it . . . OK, see you Monday . . .* Fade out; we hear his voice repeating, like a stuck gramophone record: *OK, see you Monday . . . OK, see you Monday . . .**

---

* End of reel one.

Fade in. We are in the FRIEND's apartment. He is seen in close-up, silhouetted against a window.

FRIEND lighting a cigarette: *Begin at the beginning . . . When did it happen?*

CORINNE off: *Tuesday . . . That's right, Tuesday evening after we went swimming.*

FRIEND the cigarette wagging in his lips: *You said the day before yesterday . . .*

CORINNE off: *I got it wrong. I'm sure it was Tuesday because I stopped taking the pill on Wednesday . . . and anyway, whatever happened I wasn't so scared.*

The theme music begins again and continues intermittently throughout the sequence, at times almost drowning the conversation.

FRIEND: *What would you be scared about? It wasn't the first time.*

Camera tracks out gradually to include CORINNE sitting on top of a table in the foreground, silhouetted against the light. She is wearing only a bra and pants, and fiddles nervously with her hair as she tells her story in a flat, unemotional voice.

CORINNE: *Yes but this time it wasn't at all the way it is in novels or Marie Claire . . . I don't know; his eyes were sort of fierce . . . his mouth . . . his words . . .*

FRIEND: *And so?*

CORINNE: *He started in the Mercedes . . . I told him I fancied him too much just to let him screw me . . . it would be better if we met another time . . . I mean it's idiotic, necking in cars . . . I told him he'd better take me home . . . and that I'd ring him up in the afternoon . . . I wanted a fuck but I'd rather wait.*

Camera begins to track in slowly on CORINNE, eventually cutting out the FRIEND.

FRIEND: *And what did he answer?*

CORINNE: *He talked about my body and how I turned him on, and how it was mean and vulgar.*

FRIEND: *Were you thinking of me too?*

CORINNE: *Yes, of course I was thinking of you.*

FRIEND off: *But he started by driving you home? That's what I don't understand.*

TITLE blue letters: ANAL
                                       YSIS

Resume on CORINNE in close-up, head bent, the FRIEND in the background.

CORINNE : *Yes, but we ended up stopping in the rue Molitor and we necked for a long time in the parking lot . . . He put one hand between my legs . . . he had the other round my neck . . . but without moving at all . . . We stayed like that for a long time.*

FRIEND : *What about you?*

CORINNE raising her head, still fiddling with her hair : *I didn't move either . . . I was cold . . . He guessed I felt like drinking some more . . . We went all the way to Saint-Lazare . . . all the cafés were shut.*

FRIEND : *Of course, he would go to Saint-Lazare — he lives in the rue Pasquier.*

Camera tracks out, panning slightly left, as CORINNE continues. The FRIEND puffs at his cigarette.

CORINNE : *Yes, of course . . . He . . . I was tired and terribly cold . . . I realize now that I wasn't so drunk . . . I just wanted him to fuck me, that's all. I didn't care where, really, in the lift even, but I said nothing . . . I felt his shoulder touching one of my breasts when he closed the door.*

FRIEND leaning forward : *How come?*

CORINNE : *It just happened that way . . .*

Camera tracks in on them again as she continues, propping her arm on her knees.

CORINNE : *And then Monique came to open the door; she was wearing a housecoat . . . I was surprised because I thought she'd gone off to Spain with that designer, you know who I mean . . .*

FRIEND looking up : *No, I don't know.*

CORINNE gesturing : *Yes you do . . . we saw them queueing in front of the George V cinema . . .*

FRIEND : *Oh yes, sure, but I didn't know she was his wife.*

CORINNE : *They've only been married for two months.*

Camera begins to track in again.

FRIEND : *Well, what happened next?*

CORINNE : *Well, she opened the door . . .*

We move in to a close-up of the FRIEND, cutting out CORINNE as she continues.

CORINNE off : *. . . Paul took off his coat and asked if she had anything hot to drink . . . Monique answered that there was only whisky and some revolting red wine . . . She began to laugh . . . Paul suddenly*

21

started looking uptight . . . I burst out laughing too . . . He looked at us . . . then he said he was going to change his clothes . . . I went with Monique to her room — rather nice . . . Camera moves back to show CORINNE *again . . . There was a fire on . . . I took off my mac . . . Monique was looking at me . . . She asked me why I seemed to be shivering, and said that if I was cold I could get undressed, I shouldn't feel embarrassed . . . Then she helped me.*

FRIEND : *To do what?*

CORINNE : *To take off my skirt and jumper.*

FRIEND : *Yes . . . yes.*

CORINNE : *There I was in my bra and panties* . . . She drops her legs to the ground . . . *I moved closer to the fire . . . my back was turned to her . . . I'm sure she was looking at me* . . . She raises one leg . . . *I asked her why she wasn't saying anything . . . She didn't answer so I turned round . . . She was standing by the window* . . . The FRIEND leans forward, interested . . . *Her back was turned too . . . She felt me looking at her and took off her housecoat — she was stark naked . . . She asked me if I didn't think her arse was too big . . . and I told her no . . . and she turned round, spreading her legs open* . . . Camera tracks in closer on the two of them . . . *She asked me to describe them . . . and I told her that her thighs were white and her cunt was like a big black stain above them . . . She called in Paul and then came up behind me.*

FRIEND now at the edge of frame : *What for?*

CORINNE turning towards him : *To undo my bra . . . Paul came in; he was wearing pyjamas with the jacket unbuttoned; he had a bottle of whisky with him. He made me drink some and told Monique to go on.*

Camera tracks out again.

FRIEND : *What was she doing?*

CORINNE : *Fondling my breasts.*

FRIEND : *Then what?*

CORINNE : *Paul got naked too; he showed off his cock to me . . . and asked Monique to take my panties off . . . then she made me put my head between her legs . . . like this . . . my back was turned to Paul by this time and I remember her describing my buttocks to him . . .* She props her chin on her knees . . . *he was staring at them all the time . . . then he came over and touched them with his fingers . . . and Monique was pouring the remains of the bottle onto my back . . . I could feel the wine dripping between my buttocks . . . Then*

Paul knelt down and began to lick my arse . . . It wasn't disagreeable
. . . it was really very nice . . . I could feel Monique's pussy against my
neck, and I could feel her pubic hairs mingling with my hair . . . and
while her husband fingered my buttocks, she reached down and went
on petting my breasts; she'd taken my hands and put them on her own
buttocks . . . CORINNE *fondles the* FRIEND'S *hair . . . and I could feel*
them spreading then growing tight whenever I plunged my fingers
into the cleft . . .

(Still on page 33.)

FRIEND : *And you?*

CORINNE : *They wanted me to describe it to them, to say what I was*
feeling to excite them . . . Are there only Gitanes left? Don't you have
any American cigarettes?

FRIEND : *In my jacket . . .*

CORINNE hops from the table and goes off as the FRIEND lights
another cigarette.

CORINNE off : *No, there aren't any left.*

FRIEND shaking out the match : *Have a Gitane.*

CORINNE reappears and hops back onto the table, almost obscur-
ing the FRIEND from view.

CORINNE : *No, I loathe them.*

FRIEND : *Was there any more?*

CORINNE : *After a while, Paul asked Monique to change places with*
me.

FRIEND : *With you standing and her kneeling?*

CORINNE : *That's right; she kissed my pussy while I helped Paul to*
fuck her from behind.

FRIEND : *Was that all?*

Camera tracks in again, slowly.

CORINNE : *Then we all three watched each other masturbate, and*
then suddenly Paul started shouting: ' Into the kitchen, pussies! Into
the kitchen, pussies! . . .'

FRIEND : *The kitchen? Why?*

CORINNE is by now in extreme close-up, seen from below.

CORINNE : *I'm just about to tell you — on the fridge there was a dish*
of milk, for the cat, I guess . . . She gestures with one hand . . . *' Milk*
is for pussies,' Monique said. ' How much will you bet me to squat on
the plate? ' ' Bet you wouldn't dare,' Paul said. So Monique climbed
into the sink to be at the same level as the fridge, and she squatted

23

down and dipped her bottom in the milk . . . then she ordered us to masturbate; she was watching us the whole time.

FRIEND : *Then what happened?*

CORINNE : *Just as I was starting to come, Paul cried out: ' Stop, stop,' and told me to get into the sink too; he made me kneel down in front of Monique . . .* Slow track out again . . . *Then he took an egg out of the fridge and, while I was licking Monique's pussy which was still in the milk, Paul placed the egg between my buttocks and told me to come until the egg broke and ran down between my legs.*

FRIEND stroking her leg : *Did all this really happen or was it a nightmare?*

CORINNE : *I don't remember . . .*

FRIEND : *I adore you Corinne; come and excite me!*

Fade out.

TITLE red letters :

SATURDAY   /   SATURDAY   /   SATURDAY
            10   10 A.M.

The music stops.

Fade in to the parking lot in front of the apartment block where ROLAND and CORINNE live. In the background is the red coupé we saw earlier, on the left a black Facel-Vega convertible. A twelve-year-old kid in a striped tee-shirt and Indian feathers is shooting arrows at the car . . . ROLAND and CORINNE come out of the apartment block in the background, and CORINNE pauses to rummage in her handbag.

ROLAND : *Hurry up, or there'll be a jam on the motorway.*

He hurries forward, a Gitane hanging from his lip, and chases away the kid, whose name is CHRISTOPHE.

ROLAND : *I'll do you, you little bastard!*

Pan left as he hurries over to the Facel and gets in. The kid comes over and starts yelling at him.

CHRISTOPHE : *Hey, mister, what make is this crate?*

ROLAND : *Piss off!* He slams the door.

CHRISTOPHE running round the front of the car as CORINNE appears on the other side : *I know . . . it's a crummy old Facel!* ROLAND lowers the hood. *As crummy as your wife!*

CORINNE cuffs him and gets into the car. ROLAND starts the engine as the kid runs round it bawling :

24

CHRISTOPHE : *A crummy old Facel!*
Pan right as ROLAND backs rapidly across the parking lot — and straight into the front of a Dauphine which is sitting in the corner with a bicycle on its roof.
CHRISTOPHE dancing across after them : *A crummy old Facel . . .*
He breaks off and looks at the back of the Facel. Roland opens the door.

TITLE blue letters :   SCENE
       FROM
       PARIS
       LIFE

CHRISTOPHE shouting off : *Hey, Ma, they've crashed the Dauphine!*
Resume on the scene. ROLAND gets out to inspect the damage. He kicks the front of the Dauphine a couple of times, then comes back round the front of the Facel to the driving seat.
ROLAND : *It's nothing.*
CHRISTOPHE chasing after him : *Ma, they've hit the Dauphine!*
To ROLAND : *We'll have to exchange addresses.*
ROLAND chasing him away : *I'll kick your backside!*
 CHRISTOPHE runs round the other side of the car and bawls up to his mother again.
CHRISTOPHE : *Ma! Ma!*
 ROLAND pulls a bank-note out of his pocket and goes round the back of the car.
ROLAND : *D'you want to earn 1000 francs? . . . Then belt up. O.K.?*
CHRISTOPHE pocketing the note : *Thanks . . .* Shouting : *Ma!*
 CHRISTOPHE'S MOTHER hurries down the steps from the apartment block in the background, while ROLAND takes off with a screech of tyres. She throws the tennis things she is carrying down by the Dauphine and rushes across the parking lot.
MOTHER : *Hey, 8805, stop!* Camera pans as she comes up to the Facel, which has stopped. *Look what you've done to my car!*
ROLAND : *There's nothing wrong with your car!*
 In the background, CHRISTOPHE picks up a spent arrow and takes aim at the Facel.
MOTHER gesturing at her car : *You've made a dent, there's a bump. We'll have to exchange particulars.*
 She wrenches open the door of the Facel, grabs ROLAND by the

25

arm and pulls him out.

ROLAND : *Bumpers are made for bumping!*

MOTHER shouting : *No they're not!*

ROLAND shaking free and getting back into the car : *There's nothing wrong with it.*

CHRISTOPHE hits at him with his bow and ROLAND makes a grab for him.

MOTHER circling round the car : *Just because your father-in-law happens to own the apartment block, you think you can get away with murder.*

CORINNE standing up in the passenger seat : *And just because you've got a dress from Chez Dolores, you think you can shit on everyone else . . .* To ROLAND : *Come on.*

The MOTHER pulls ROLAND out of the car again and grabs him in a half nelson.

MOTHER : *We're going to exchange particulars.* She screams for her husband : *Georges! Georges!*

CORINNE gets out and runs round the back of the car.

ROLAND pointing as he struggles to get free : *Give me that spray-paint thing in the boot.*

CORINNE gets the boot open and ROLAND shakes free from the MOTHER.

MOTHER : *Georges! Georges!* To CORINNE : *You stuck-up little arse-hole!*

CORINNE grabs her by the wrists from behind and pulls her backwards across the parking lot. Camera pans with them as ROLAND follows, covering the helpless MOTHER with paint from an aerosol he has got out of the boot, while CHRISTOPHE dances round them as it it were a game of cowboys and Indians. (Production still on page 33.)

MOTHER shouting : *Georges! Georges!*

ROLAND spraying her : *So we're stuck-up little arse-holes are we? So we're stuck-up little arse-holes are we?*

CORINNE letting go of the MOTHER : *Oh forget it.*

She walks back to the car while ROLAND continues to spray the MOTHER with paint; then he turns the spray on the Dauphine as the MOTHER picks up a tennis racquet and starts pelting him with tennis balls.

MOTHER shouting : *Hey, cut it out . . . Georges! Georges! Georges!*

GEORGES appears on the steps of the apartment block in the background, brandishing a shotgun. He looses off one barrel at ROLAND who bolts for his car off-screen; we hear him drive off with a squeal of tyres as GEORGES races down the steps, towing a spaniel on a lead; he hands the lead to CHRISTOPHE and camera pans as he hurries across the parking lot, takes aim at the departing car and fires.

CHRISTOPHE yelling off : *Bastard! Shit-face! Communist!*
Fade out.

TITLE blue letters :   WEEKEND
    alternating rapidly with
TITLE red letters :   SATURDAY
                      11 A.M.

We are on a main road in the country; there is an ear-splitting sound of car-horns which continues throughout the following sequence. Camera pans with the Facel as ROLAND races up the middle of the road and cuts into a gap in a slow-moving queue of cars. They all hoot angrily . . . ROLAND pulls out again and moves along the outside of the queue. All the cars are now stationary and drivers and passengers are passing the time as best they can; they look up, gesturing and swearing at ROLAND and CORINNE as they pass, camera tracking slowly with the Facel . . . Two men are playing cards on the boot-lid of a black Peugeot; in the front of it a man is standing up through the sunroof, playing ball with a boy in an open 2CV ahead of them . . . We pan ahead of the Facel to a crashed car lying upside down on the opposite side of the road. A crowd of kids run along by the roadside, shouting and fooling about. Sound of a car radio. Another car jerks a few feet forward to stop the Facel getting into a space. More furious hooting . . . ROLAND almost makes it into a space in front of the 2CV but the driver gets out and several more people gather round and start shouting and swearing at the couple . . . They pass a travelling menagerie — monkeys and lions on a couple of trucks and a llama looking out over the countryside. ROLAND drives on up the middle of the road, everyone shouting and hooting at him as he passes. Music.

TITLE red letters :   1.40 P.M.

     Camera tracks past an empty bus, a couple of passengers leaning against the side of it.

TITLE blue letters :   WEEKEND

Resume on the bus.

TITLE red letters :   2.10 P.M.

Rapid pan as ROLAND comes to a halt on the outside of a horse and cart; everyone gathers round, shouting abuse, while a party of schoolchildren pass on the other side of the road. Camera tracks on past two more men playing ball from their open cars, past a Dauphine which has smashed into a tree in the foreground . . . ROLAND crams into a space in front of a black Panhard; the angry driver taps him on the back bumper; everyone gets out and a furious altercation starts. Music as we track on again, past a vast red and yellow Shell tanker, nose to nose with a white Fiat coupé. (Still on page 34.) The Facel passes on the outside; a car goes by in the opposite direction . . . Two people are playing chess on the road behind their car . . . More hooting and yelling as ROLAND drives on up the middle of the road. He is finally brought to a halt by an aged Simca with its doors wide open, blocking the road. CORINNE gets out and furiously slams the offside door, enraging its elderly woman driver . . . We pass two more men playing cards on a car bonnet. They break off their game to hurl abuse at ROLAND and CORINNE as they move past. A little further on, a man clad in orange oilskins is hauling up the sails on his yacht, which is mounted on a trailer . . . ROLAND keeps trying to find a space, but no-one will let him in. He finally makes it because the driver of one car has been urinating in the ditch; buttoning up his fly, the man waves an angry fist over his shoulder . . . The queue begins to move and we pass the scene of the hold-up : a motorcycle policeman is beckoning the traffic past a multiple smash; crumpled cars are being towed away; there is blood on the road and bodies lie strewn in the ditch. (Still on page 34.) Camera pans with the Facel as it takes a right-hand turn off the main road, then speeds away into the distance between ploughed fields. Fade out.*

---

* End of reel two.

Fade in on the car entering a small town. Camera pans as it rounds a corner, hooting, sweeps round a small square knocking over a dustbin and comes to a halt in front of a shop. A FARMER, singing lustily at the wheel of his tractor, drives across the square and off to the left. ROLAND and CORINNE are seen through the windscreen of the stationary car. The FARMER is heard singing away as he drives on across the square. There is the sound of a high-revving engine, then CORINNE suddenly leaps out of the passenger seat and we see her reflection in the windscreen as she urgently flags down an approaching car. The roar of the engine stops in a splintering crash; there is a deathly silence. CORINNE reappears and gets back into the Facel, while ROLAND, unmoved, takes a hairbrush from the glove-box and brushes his hair in the rear-view mirror. CORINNE turns on the radio, then starts tidying herself.

ROLAND : *Well, go on and telephone, then. Go and telephone to Oinville.*

CORINNE in a shaken voice : *If you drove a bit faster we'd be on time. You never use the overdrive.*

ROLAND : *Yeah, well I'll drive just the way I damn well please.*

CORINNE glancing off-screen : *It's just that we don't want Mummy to call for an ambulance rather than us, that's all.*

ROLAND : *Fucking nuisance, the lot of them.*

CORINNE takes her hairbrush and twists the rear-view mirror so that she can see into it.

CORINNE brushing her hair : *Yeah, I know, but if Daddy takes along his little Japanese tape-recorder and dictates another will . . .*

ROLAND : *That's illegal, anyway.*

CORINNE : *Sure, but if you want to spend the winter in Mexico you'd better play it safe or else you'll find yourself spending it in the clink.*

ROLAND : *Of course we won't spend it in the clink. Come on, sweetie, stop worrying. It'll all work out O.K.*

He puts his arm round her and kisses her on the cheek. She turns away.

CORINNE : *Then why have we been sweating it out for the past five years putting poison in his mashed potato every Saturday?*

A girl — JULIET — is heard shouting off-screen.

JULIET off : *My special Chrysler engine . . .*

The couple glance in her direction.

ROLAND : *Then ring them, say there's been a diversion. Tell them the motorway's blocked and we've been delayed.*

CORINNE : *Did you see the Triumph?* She turns to ROLAND. *If only that could have been Mummy and Daddy, it would have made everything a whole lot easier.*

JULIET and the FARMER are yelling at one another off-screen.

JULIET off : *I've got witnesses!*

FARMER off : *Will you shut up you little bitch!*

JULIET off : *You bastard of a peasant!*

CORINNE gets out of the car and goes to telephone; ROLAND lights a cigarette and turns up the car radio.

In a high angle shot we see the driver of the crashed car, lying dead in his seat, wearing a pair of green sunglasses. His head is thrown back and his chest and face are covered in blood.

FARMER shouting off : *Little bourgeois cunt!*

The dead driver is seen from another angle; there is blood all over the windscreen in front of him and the wheel of the tractor can be seen in the background.

JULIET off : *You stinking great field rat!*

Loud music.

TITLE blue letters :

				THE
SS	/	SS	/	CLASS
		STRUGGLE		STRUGGLE

FARMER off : *Little Parisian tart!*

We see the crashed car from above, the blood-covered corpse of the driver lying back, staring up at camera.

JULIET off : *You'd have done better to stay in your pigsty instead of coming here and killing the man I love!*

JULIET stands in front of an advertisement hoarding, nervously sucking the end of her sunglasses. The Esso tiger leers over her shoulder. (Still on page 35.)

FARMER off : *He had no business driving so fast. This is the Ile de France, not Saint-Tropez.*

Three men — peasants or garage hands — stand in front of the advertisement hoarding with its pop-art colours, watching impassively as JULIET screams at the FARMER off-screen. Music. A plane flies overhead, almost drowning her hysterical voice.

JULIET screaming off : *You fucking bastard! It makes you sick that we've got money and you haven't, doesn't it? You're pissed off 'cause we go and fuck on the Riviera and you don't, and then we move on to Megève in the winter . . . You get really cheesed off seeing us spend all that lolly all the year round . . .*

Medium shot of the accident : the car, a red Triumph two-seater, has smashed into the side of the tractor and ridden up over its front wheels. Blood oozes over the ground beneath it. JULIET — big-breasted with long black hair, her chic green sweater and yellow pants covered with blood — advances towards the tractor, screaming at the FARMER. (Still on page 35.)

JULIET . . . *going to Greece in the spring. Over there they just throw shit-hole peasants like you into gaol along with their fucking tractors . . .*

Camera pans with her as she starts hysterically kicking the back wheel of the tractor. This last insult is too much for the FARMER, and he scrambles out of his cab, clutching an enormous French sandwich.

FARMER : *Now, miss, you've no right to insult my tractor!*

He advances towards her threateningly and she backs away, still swearing.

JULIET : *Your tractor! I bet you don't even own it and it belongs to one of those rotten unions or to some fucking co-operative.* She disappears round the back of the tractor.

FARMER pointing an accusing finger : *And that foreign car of yours, I bet you stole it!*

Resume on the dead driver in the Triumph.

JULIET off : *No I did not! The heir to the Robert factories gave it to me because I let him fuck me . . .*

We see a couple standing in front of the advertisement hoarding, looking on. The man has his arm round the girl and grins faintly as JULIET continues screaming.

JULIET off : *Yeah, but your bunch doesn't have any balls, you can't even fuck; why, it's the government which fucks you with all your stinking, shitty tractors . . .*

FARMER off : Even so, if it weren't for me and my tractor, the French would have nothing to eat.

JULIET off : *I don't give a damn, I don't give a damn! Paul's dead!*

31

FARMER off : *No bread, no wheat, no oats . . .*
JULIET off : *I don't give a fuck!*
FARMER off : *. . . no rye, no maize, no beetroot . . .*
JULIET off : *I don't care! I don't care! I don't care! I don't care! . . .*
The man puffs at his cigarette — he is clearly enjoying the spectacle.
Another shot of PAUL lying dead in the Triumph.
JULIET off : *. . . It was his right of way and now he's dead!*
FARMER off : *His right of way? His right of way? Don't be too sure about that!*
JULIET off : *Yes, he had the right of way . . .*
A long-faced man in overalls and a red cap is seen standing in front of the Esso tiger. He blinks. (Still on page 36.)
JULIET off : *He was young, handsome, rich — that gave him right of way over everyone, over the fat, over the . . . over the poor . . .*
ROLAND stands watching in front of the red and yellow hoarding.
JULIET off : *. . . over the old, over the . . .*
FARMER off : *You're not to say that, Miss!*
JULIET mimicking him, off : *You're not to say that, Miss! . . .*
PAUL's corpse lies staring up at camera through its green sunglasses.
JULIET off : *. . . You great lump of shit! You great lump of shit!*
A man in a khaki jacket and baseball cap is seen in front of the hoarding. He begins to heave with silent laughter as the FARMER and JULIET scream at one another.
FARMER off : *Why, you little bitch!*
JULIET off : *You and your tractor, your cheap old tractor!*
Sound of her kicking the tractor.
FARMER off : *One million four hundred thousand — that's plenty if you have to work with your own hands.*
JULIET off : *Your stinking, shitty, old tractor . . .*
Back to the scene of the crash. JULIET beats her hands in rage on the crumpled front of the Triumph. The FARMER munches his sandwich.
JULIET : *. . . What about my Triumph — two and a half million with its special Chrysler engine; and now it's a write-off and you don't care, do you? It's a write-off I tell you . . .*
FARMER : *So what?*
JULIET : *And now he's dead . . .* Coming towards him : *And you*

32

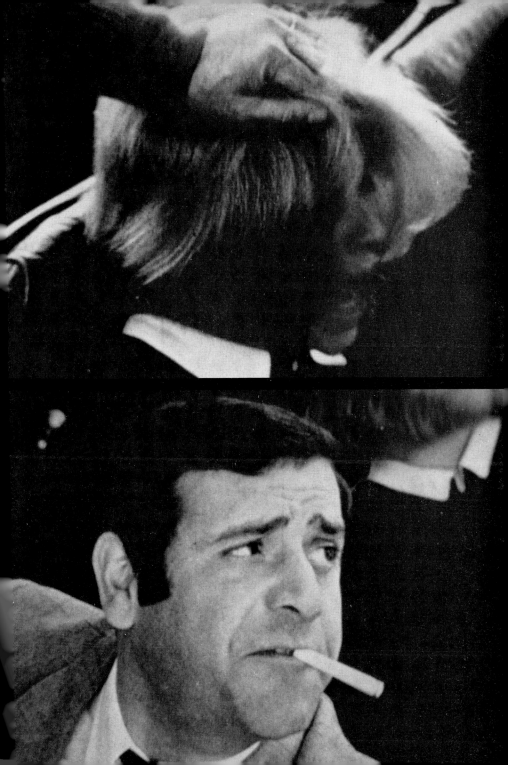

*needn't think you're going to get away with it. You won't get away
with it.* She starts hitting him. *I'll make damn sure you don't!*
Resume on the man in the baseball cap. He grins as the Farmer
shouts.

Farmer off : *Will you shut up, you little bitch!*
Juliet off : *There's some witnesses . . . Monsieur, Monsieur, it was
our right of way, wasn't it?*
The Facel's horn sounds off-screen.
Corinne and Roland are inside the car. The Farmer opens the
passenger door while Juliet hurries round the other side.
Corinne : *Please . . . we're already late . . .*
Camera pans round in a semi-circle as Roland drives off, sound-
ing his horn. Juliet and the Farmer rush after the car, shouting.
Farmer : *You can't leave just like that! Aren't we all brothers like
Marx said? Bastards! Bastards!*
The car drives away off-screen.
Juliet screaming after it : *Jews! Filthy, rotten, stinking Jews!*
The Farmer puts a comforting arm round her. She gives a little
sigh of despair and sinks her head against his chest. They walk
away, arm in arm. (Still on page 36.) Fade out.

Title blue letters :   COUNTER
                              FEITO
                              GRAPHY

Posed as if for a formal photograph, the various spectators of the
previous scene stand grouped in front of the pop-art advertisement hoarding. Corinne is absent, but in the centre stands
Roland, one hand in his pocket, his other arm round the blood-
stained Juliet. Loud music.

Title blue and red figures :   9 5 2

                              4 9 $\frac{K}{M}$

The figures in the bottom row flick up to 61.
We see Corinne from behind — camera is on the back of the
open car — as Roland drives furiously through the countryside.
Corinne to Roland off-screen : *You and your fucking short cuts!
They do nothing but lose us time . . .*
Roland off, to another motorist : *Keep to the right, you!*

41

CORINNE turning to him angrily : . . . *And that means money too.*
ROLAND off : *Cut it out, Corinne!*
She looks round at the countryside.
CORINNE : *When did civilisation begin?*
ROLAND hoots.
ROLAND off : *Why d'you want to know? Does it bother you?*
CORINNE looking about her : *No, it's the landscape . . .* ROLAND
changes gear . . . *Anyway, I don't understand.*
ROLAND off : *What?*
CORINNE : *You heard what he said just now? 'Aren't we all brothers,
like Marx said?'*
ROLAND off, as they round a bend : *It wasn't Marx, it was Jesus —
another Commie.*
CORINNE : *I don't know; anyway you're right. Even if it's true, who
cares? We're not living in the Middle Ages . . . What's the time?*

TITLE red letters :

SATURDAY	/	SATURDAY	/	SATURDAY
		3		3 P.M.

There is hooting and furious shouting off.
High angle close-up of CORINNE in the passenger seat, shouting
and waving her hands. A hand reaches down and grabs her by
the hair, shaking her violently. (Still on page 37.) She grabs the
hand and bites it; there is a scream. Other people are heard yelling.

TITLE red letters :

SATURDAY	/	SATURDAY	/	SATURDAY
		4		4 P.M.

More hooting as CORINNE is heard shouting :
CORINNE off : *Get a move on up front! . . . Silly buggers!*
We now see ROLAND from above with CORINNE fighting someone
in the background. He turns and yells up at someone off-screen.
(Still on page 37.)
ROLAND : *If I fuck your wife and it hurts her, would you call that a
scratch? . . . Well then . . . you bastards!*
Another hand reaches down and hits him. He grabs it and bites
the arm.
Resume on CORINNE glaring up at her attacker. She turns and
settles herself angrily in her seat.

42

CORINNE furious : *Run them over!*

TITLE blue and red figures :   9 5 2

$$7\ 8\ \begin{matrix} K \\ M \end{matrix}$$

The figures in the bottom row flick up to 88.

CORINNE is seen through the windscreen of the moving car. She looks up at the sky and wraps a long yellow scarf round her neck.

CORINNE : *D'you think it's going to rain?*

ROLAND changes up and accelerates.

ROLAND off : *Of course it's going to rain.*

CORINNE looking up at the sky again : *I don't think so. The sun's shining.*

ROLAND off : *It's going to rain I tell you. Now shut up.*

She looks at him.

TITLE red letters :   SATURDAY
                              5 P.M.

The sound of the car engine continues over; then we hear hooting.

Another road : it is pouring with rain. Two crashed cars lie in the ditch. A girl in a red raincoat and white boots, with a white-painted face, runs into the middle of the road, waving her arms. The Facel comes up, hooting, and stops.

MARIE-MADELEINE running up to the passenger door : *Can you give me a lift?* She runs round the front of the car as ROLAND gets out, repeating : *Well, can you give me a lift?*

ROLAND walks round her suspiciously, lifts up her raincoat to see what she's got on underneath, then beckons her into the car with a jerk of his thumb. He goes back to open the car door while the girl calls to a friend, who emerges from one of the wrecked cars on the opposite side of the road.

MARIE-MADELEINE : *Joseph! Joseph!*

A strange figure — JOSEPH BALSAMO — emerges from the wrecked car, wearing a red coat and a trilby hat and brandishing a branch of greenery. He runs across the road.

JOSEPH : *Are you going to Mont-Saint-Gely?*

ROLAND pointing back down the road : *Mont-Saint-Gely's that way, not this way.*

43

JOSEPH : *Then go back that way.*
ROLAND : *Why the hell should I?*
JOSEPH pulling out a gun : *Turn her round!*
ROLAND starting to get into the car : *Piss off.*
JOSEPH swiping at him with the branch : *Come on!*
> The two men continue to shout at one another for a moment, then JOSEPH suddenly looses off a shot from his gun.

JOSEPH : *Come on, turn her round.*
> He bundles MARIE-MADELEINE into the back seat and shoves ROLAND in through the door after her.

JOSEPH : *Come on, quick! Get a move on there!*
> He walks round the other side of the car and forces ROLAND to make a three-point turn, waving his branch and shooting, like a lion tamer with a tricky animal. (Still on page 38.)

JOSEPH yelling : *Come on, move!* The car shoots across the road. He beats it on the bonnet with the branch and yells : *Stop!*
> ROLAND backs it round again, JOSEPH shouting *Gently! Gently!* as he does so. Then JOSEPH hauls open the passenger door and grabs CORINNE by the arm, forcing her to get out.

JOSEPH : *Come on, out you get!*
> She protests wildly as he gets into the back seat and forces her to get in again in front of him.

JOSEPH to ROLAND : *Now get a move on.*
> CORINNE shuts the door. Loud music. Camera pans as the car turns and roars off up the road into the pouring rain. Fade out.

TITLE blue letters :

| THE | / | THE EX | / | THE EXTERMIN |
| ANGEL | | ANGEL | | ATING ANGEL |

> The music continues over.
> We now see the two couples through the windscreen of the moving car. It has stopped raining and the hood is down. JOSEPH turns from side to side, taking photographs of CORINNE and ROLAND, while ROLAND hoots and shouts wildly at passing motorists, trying to attract their attention.

ROLAND waving : *Help!*
CORINNE : *What's the point of taking all these photos?*
JOSEPH putting down the camera and taking the gun from the girl : *Silence! It's for the Ministry of the Interior — even God has his police.*

ROLAND turning slightly towards him : *Well, we've got nothing to fear.*

JOSEPH threateningly : *Well prove it, then — come on, quick.*

ROLAND sounds his horn again and he and CORINNE both wave wildly at another passing motorist.

ROLAND and CORINNE in chorus : *Help! Help!*

JOSEPH levelling his gun at ROLAND : *Silence, I said! Silence!* Then, after a pause : *Come on, prove it, quick!*

ROLAND and CORINNE waving and shouting again : *Help! Help!*

JOSEPH takes a shot at the passing car.

JOSEPH : *Will you shut up! Will you shut up now!*

There is a silence as the Facel accelerates up the road between an avenue of poplar trees. Then ROLAND half turns and says :

ROLAND : *What proof?*

JOSEPH unbuttons his shirt but does not reply. ROLAND begins to bluster a little as if trying to justify himself.

ROLAND : *Well, I don't know . . . I fuck her legally, we're married. I bet you can't say the same about you and your bird.*

CORINNE emphatically : *I agree entirely.*

JOSEPH : *Very well. Tell me your name, Madame.*

CORINNE surprised : *My name's Corinne Durand.*

JOSEPH : *No it isn't. That's your husband's name. What's yours?*

CORINNE : *My maiden name is Corinne Vitron.*

JOSEPH : *No, that's your father's name. What's yours?*

CORINNE shrugging : *What? . . . My name? . . . Well, I . . .*

JOSEPH : *That just shows. You see, you don't even know who you are. Christianity is the refusal to know oneself. It's the death of language.*

ROLAND sounds his horn again.

ROLAND and CORINNE shouting and waving : *Help!*

JOSEPH : *I told you to keep quiet. Will you shut up? Are you going to keep your mouths shut now?*

CORINNE turning to JOSEPH : *Well, what's your name?*

JOSEPH hands his gun to the girl as he replies.

JOSEPH : *Joseph Balsamo.*

ROLAND rounding a bend : *Never heard of him.*

CORINNE : *Me neither.*

ROLAND sounds his horn and they both start shouting and waving again.

CORINNE and ROLAND hysterically : *Help!*

Music.

45

JOSEPH whipping out his gun again : *Will you shut up?* A pause. *Listen, I'm not surprised, with mugs like yours. You look like something out of the* Reader's Digest.

ROLAND hooting, shouting and waving : *Help!*

JOSEPH : *Quiet please. You remind me of those removal men who refused to give André Breton a lift when he was dying . . . Anyway I'll explain. Joseph Balsamo is the son of God and of Alexandre Dumas. Everyone knows God's an old queer. Well he buggered Dumas and here I am as a result . . . I'm God. Yes, I'm God . . . because I'm lazy.*

> MARIE-MADELEINE shouts over his shoulder as ROLAND starts waving and hooting again.

MARIE-MADELEINE : *That's not true, beloved.*

CORINNE shrieking hysterically over and over again : *Help! Help! Help!*

JOSEPH : *Will you shut up, once and for all?* He finally silences her by taking a shot at the passing car. *Listen . . . shut up, Marie-Madeleine.* To the others : *She's a nice bird, but she doesn't understand a thing. Laziness . . . God . . .*

ROLAND and CORINNE shouting and waving : *Help!*

JOSEPH silencing them with another gunshot : *Will you please shut up! I said shut up; that's enough for now, get it? . . . She's a good girl. She understands laziness. She understands God, too. I have only to command, and she obeys.*

CORINNE : *But what exactly do you do?*

JOSEPH : *I am here to proclaim to these Modern Times the end of the grammatical era and the beginning of an age of flamboyance in every field, especially that of the cinema.*

ROLAND slowing down : *Yeah, well I've had enough. I'm stopping.*

JOSEPH : *Don't do that. Be a sport. Listen, I'll make a deal with you —if you drive me to London I'll give you whatever you want.*

CORINNE contemptuously : *Oh sure, a seedy tramp like you!*

JOSEPH pointing : *No, I promise, look under the dashboard. Take a good look. There . . .*

> CORINNE reaches under the dashboard and pulls out a struggling white rabbit. She holds it up by the ears.

CORINNE in wonder : *Shit, a miracle!*

ROLAND looking at it with a slightly baffled expression : *A rabbit!*

JOSEPH : *You see — anything you want on condition you take me to*

London.

ROLAND : *A Mercedes . . . a big sports Mercedes?*

JOSEPH : *O.K.*

CORINNE : *A Saint-Laurent evening dress?*

JOSEPH : *O.K.*

ROLAND : *A hotel on Miami beach?*

JOSEPH : *Hmmm . . .*

CORINNE excitedly : *Turn me into a blonde — a real one, O.K.?*

ROLAND : *A fleet of Mirage IVs like the yids used to wipe out the wogs?*

CORINNE : *A weekend with James Bond?*

ROLAND with a gleam in his eye : *Yeah, me too . . .* He brings the car to a halt.

JOSEPH : *Is that really all you want?*

ROLAND : *Sure, it'll do . . .*

MARIE-MADELEINE levels the gun at CORINNE.

JOSEPH contemptuously : *You poor goons! What a pair of bastards! You won't get a thing from me.*

CORINNE suddenly grabs the gun from MARIE-MADELEINE and levels it at JOSEPH.

CORINNE : *Come on, quick, a miracle! Come on you crook, a miracle!*

JOSEPH : *D'you really think I'm going to perform for a couple of arse-holes like you?*

ROLAND with a jerk of his head : *O.K., that'll do. Now get out!*

CORINNE waving the gun at them : *Come on, out!**

Long shot of a field littered with crashed cars — the stationary Facel on the road in the distance.

CORINNE getting out of the car : *Come on, come on, get out! Buzz off!* They all get out of the car and CORINNE and ROLAND begin to chase the other two across the field towards us, shouting and hurling abuse at them. ROLAND keeps punching JOSEPH, who tries to fend him off with his branch, while CORINNE chases after MARIE-MADELEINE, firing off shots from the gun.

ROLAND to MARIE-MADELEINE : *Out, you little tart, I'll teach you. I'll make you run . . .* To CORINNE : *Go on, shoot 'em down, shoot!* Hitting JOSEPH : *Dirty Jew! Shit! Bastard! Turd! Just you wait. I'll show you . . .*

---

* End of reel three.

47

Loud music. Suddenly JOSEPH halts by a ruined car and raises his hands in the air. CORINNE stands a little way away, levelling the gun at him.

JOSEPH : *Silence!*

Another shot of the same scene. The cars have now disappeared and instead a flock of sheep are trotting past, so that CORINNE and JOSEPH are seen amongst a sea of white backs. JOSEPH raises his arms in the air again and advances on CORINNE.

JOSEPH : *Silence!*

He suddenly grabs the gun from her and trains it on her and ROLAND, who has just appeared on the left. (Still on page 38.) Camera pans as JOSEPH chases them back across the field towards the car, scourging them with his branch. The flock of sheep scatter on either side.

JOSEPH : *Vade retro, vade retro . . . Go home, go home . . . go home, go home . . .*

TITLE blue and red figures :   9 5 7

$$2\ 3\ \frac{K}{M}$$

The figures in the bottom row flick up to 35.

CORINNE and ROLAND are on the road again, seen through the windscreen of the moving car. The music continues. CORINNE puts on her sunglasses and says :

CORINNE : *You see, the sun's come out.*

A car coming in the other direction hoots. ROLAND has to swerve suddenly and pass it on the wrong side.

ROLAND yelling : *Keep to your lane!*

CORINNE simultaneously : *Moron!*

In a high angle shot, camera pans with the car seen through some trees as it accelerates round a bend and goes on up the road, hooting.

Another high angle shot : the Facel comes towards us, hooting wildly at a cyclist who is swerving around in the middle of the road.

CYCLIST : *Long live Anquetil! Up Poulidor!*

Camera pans with the car as it moves past, finally forcing the cyclist off the road; he crashes head first into a ditch. We hear the Facel hooting, then a breakdown lorry towing a crashed car moves past in the opposite direction.

We are now moving ahead of the Facel as it speeds along the road. Hooting loudly, it forces a Simca into the ditch. Music as it rounds a bend, then drives straight at a pedestrian, forcing him to leap off the road . . . It nearly leaves the road itself as a vast yellow bulldozer moves past in the opposite direction; then it drives on, running over a chicken.

Reverse shot: there is a massive pile-up on the road ahead. Crumpled cars are burning with bright orange flames.

Resume on the Facel as it narrowly misses another fowl.

Flash of the burning cars: there are bodies strewn around.

Resume on the Facel accelerating.

Back to the cars.

The Facel suddenly swerves.

Shot of the blazing cars ahead.

Resume on the Facel swerving.

Back to the blazing pile-up. The Facel's horn sounds for several seconds and then all is quiet. ROLAND crawls out from underneath one of the blazing wrecks, his shirt covered in blood. CORINNE is having hysterics on the other side of it. (Still on page 39.)

CORINNE standing up and screaming: *Heeelllp! My Hermès bag!*

Thick black smoke rises from the burning wrecks.

TITLE blue letters: FROM THE FRENCH
                       REVOLUTION TO
                       U N R WEEKENDS

A voice is heard declaiming loudly off-screen.

SAINT-JUST off: *Freedom, like crime, is born of violence . . .*

Camera tracks slowly with ROLAND and CORINNE as they walk along a path across a field. Jean-Pierre Léaud, dressed as SAINT-JUST in a long coat and cocked hat, accompanies them, declaiming loudly from a book in his hand.

SAINT-JUST: *. . . It is as though it were the virtue which springs from vice . . .*

CORINNE shouting to ROLAND ahead of her: *Is the knife under the cushion?* The track loses her.

SAINT-JUST: *. . . fighting in desperation against slavery.*

ROLAND shouting back to CORINNE: *No, it's in the outhouse.*

49

SAINT-JUST : *The struggle will be long and freedom will kill freedom. Can one truly conceive that inconsistent humanity* . . .
ROLAND to CORINNE off-screen : *What about the axe?*
SAINT-JUST : *Can one believe that man created society* . . . CORINNE reappears . . . *in order to be happy and reasonable therein?* Tearing off his red-cockaded hat : *No!*

He halts and advances towards camera while the couple plod on along the path in the background. (Still on page 39.)
SAINT-JUST : *One is led to assume that, weary of the restfulness and wisdom of Nature* . . . He halts.
CORINNE shouting to ROLAND : *Same place!*
SAINT-JUST advancing towards camera again : . . . *he wishes to be unhappy and mad! I see only constitutions which are backed by gold, pride and blood and nowhere do I see* . . . He turns towards the departing figures of ROLAND and CORINNE . . . *gentle humanity* . . . He starts to follow them . . . *the fairness and moderation which ought to form the basis of the social treaty.*

Camera cranes up, then begins to track after him. Fade out.

TITLE red letters :   SU
                                 ND
                                 AY

Camera pans with CORINNE and ROLAND as they walk along by the roadside. We hear a voice singing.
YOUNG MAN off : *I'm calling out in the emptiness.*

TITLE blue and red letters :   STORY
                                FOR
                                MONDAY

Resume on SAINT-JUST declaiming.
SAINT-JUST : . . . *of the social treaty.*
Fade out.

TITLE red letters :   SU
                                 ND
                                 AY

The sequence starts again : pan with the couple as they walk along by the roadside.
YOUNG MAN singing off : *I'm calling out in the emptiness.*

50

TITLE blue and red letters :   STORY
FOR
MONDAY

We see the panning shot for the third time, but it now continues
as the couple walk up to a yellow phone booth at the roadside,
where Jean-Pierre Léaud, now dressed as a YOUNG MAN, is singing into the telephone.

YOUNG MAN :

I'm calling out in the emptiness,
I'm calling to you in the night.
My words are hurried and breathless . . .

The couple bang on the window.

ROLAND : *Hurry up in there!*

CORINNE goes off while ROLAND stands with his back to us, urinating in the ditch. As the YOUNG MAN continues to sing into the
phone, we move past the booth to a red Honda two-seater, with
the hood down, parked nearby. The couple circle round it, inspecting it.

YOUNG MAN :

. . . Will they reach you today all right?
Hallo, hallo, can you hear me?
Are your skies clear and sunny down there?
Even in the rain, a breath
Of the Esterel reaches me here.
I'm shut up here in the phone booth,
It's a cage of glass for me.
And I can see you in a bar-booth
With a view looking out on the sea.
Hallo, hallo, can you hear me?
How are Laurent . . .

ROLAND sits in the driving seat of the Honda, while CORINNE goes
back and taps on the window of the phone booth.

CORINNE off : *Excuse me . . .*

YOUNG MAN off : *. . . Jean-Luc and Joelle?*

We follow ROLAND as he gets out of the car and comes back to
the booth, which has most of its windows broken. Its door is wide
open, but ROLAND and CORINNE stand on either side looking in
through the windows and urging the YOUNG MAN to hurry up.

51

Young Man singing :

> *Tell me, do your friends still go to the islands,*
> *Fishing for mack-er-el?*
> *We've used up four units already . . .*

Roland knocking on the window : *Get a move on, can't you?*

The Young Man's delivery gets more and more feverish as they pester him.

Young Man singing :

> *There go the pips again . . .*
> *You know that I'm calling you constantly . . .*
> *Is everything still all right?*
> *What is your voice hiding from me?*
> *With whom are you dancing tonight?*

Corinne and Roland swap sides and Corinne knocks on the window.

Corinne : *Monsieur . . .*

Young Man gesticulating and singing at the top of his voice :

> *Hallo, hallo, can you hear me?*
> *Can you hear me, where are your lips?*

Corinne louder : *Monsieur . . .*

Roland : *Hey kid, this isn't the Drugstore!*

Young Man singing as loud as he can :

> *Hallo, speak louder. Will you be there*
> *If I call you back? There go the pips.*

Corinne reaches in through one of the windows which has no glass in it and grabs the Young Man by the shoulder.

Corinne shouting : *Monsieur!*

Young Man thrusting her away, still singing loudly into the phone :

> *I'm afraid I've got to hang up now.*
> *There's some people outside, they can't wait . . .*

Roland beckons to Corinne and they both disappear towards the car.

Young Man :

> *I'm afraid I have spoken too quickly,*
> *I haven't said everything yet . . .*
> *Hallo, hallo, can you hear me?*
> *They're still in a hurry outside . . .*

Roland starts the engine of the Honda and revs it up off-screen.

Young Man :

In this crazy rat-race, people don't give a damn
For a love that's laid down and died ...

On these last words he hangs up and rushes out of the booth across to the car.

YOUNG MAN angrily, to ROLAND : *Leave my little Japanese alone.*

CORINNE rushes towards the phone booth.

ROLAND : *I'm trying the gears. Is that a Porsche gearbox you've got?*

The YOUNG MAN grabs him by the shoulders and pulls him out of the car.

YOUNG MAN : *What's that to you? Push off, will you. Leave my car alone!* He pushes him away.

CORINNE calling from the phone booth off-screen : *They've only got the Paris directory here ...*

ROLAND walks round the front of the car while the YOUNG MAN starts the engine.

ROLAND : *Can you give us a ride to the nearest garage?*

YOUNG MAN revving up the engine as CORINNE reappears : *No, I've only got one seat. Your wife can come if you like, but not you.*

ROLAND pointing : *I'll get in the back.*

YOUNG MAN shouting angrily : *No you won't, you'll ruin my hood!*

ROLAND takes no notice and sits on the back of the car while CORINNE gets into the passenger seat. The YOUNG MAN stops the engine and leaps out.

YOUNG MAN : *For Chrissake get lost, will you!*

He opens the boot, pulls out the starting handle and waves it furiously at ROLAND.

YOUNG MAN : *Push off! Go on, push off!*

ROLAND : *He's nuts.*

YOUNG MAN pushing him away : *Get lost or I'll smash your face in. Go on, piss off!*

ROLAND protests while CORINNE gets out of the car. The YOUNG MAN chases her round it, picks up his spare wheel which is lying on the grass nearby and advances on the couple, threatening them with the starting handle and wheel as though they were a sword and shield. (Still on page 40.)

YOUNG MAN : *Go on, go on! Piss off! Piss off!* He finally throws the wheel at ROLAND, hitting him on the leg.

ROLAND : *He's completely nuts!*

CORINNE : *He's crazy ...*

53

YOUNG MAN as they start back towards him : *O.K. now fuck off!*
CORINNE running up : *But Monsieur, only just now you said I could come with you . . .* She gets into the passenger seat.
YOUNG MAN who has also got in : *You can if you want to.* To ROLAND : *But you stay here.*

CORINNE suddenly hits him on the head, then grabs him round the shoulders as he starts up and revs the engine urgently.
CORINNE : *Roland! Quick, Roland!*

ROLAND rushes up and pulls the YOUNG MAN out of the car.
YOUNG MAN struggling : *Let me go!*

They drag him out and frog-march him away from the car, all shouting simultaneously.
CORINNE : *Wait a moment!*
ROLAND : *Hold him by the neck!*
YOUNG MAN : *Let me go!*
ROLAND : *Turn him round!*
YOUNG MAN : *Let me go!*
ROLAND : *Hang on to him while I start her up.*

Leaving CORINNE holding the YOUNG MAN by the neck, he rushes back and leaps into the car, starts the engine and revs it furiously. Meanwhile the YOUNG MAN breaks free and throws CORINNE to to the ground.
CORINNE shouting : *No! No!*

He kicks her a few times, then rushes back to pull ROLAND out of the car.
CORINNE getting up in the background : *Help!*
ROLAND as the YOUNG MAN hauls him backward by the neck : *Police!*

The YOUNG MAN finally throws him to the ground and gives him a vicious punch to the spine, then scuttles back to the car, leaps in and wildly revs the engine. Fade out.

Loud music over a shot of wrecked cars blazing on either side of a road. There are bright orange flames, clouds of black smoke; the wrecks crackle and bang as their petrol tanks explode. Camera cranes up as ROLAND and CORINNE limp into view in the background.
ROLAND addressing a corpse lying in the road : *Hey, you, where's the nearest garage?*

Camera tracks with them as they come towards us. There are

bodies strewn everywhere. (Still on page 40.)

CORINNE addressing another one : *Is this the way to Oinville?*

ROLAND with a gesture of disgust : *These buggers are all dead.*

They both walk off down the road. Camera moves back over the bodies and blazing cars. Fade out.

Fade in on a bit of road with a wall in the background, framed by trees. The music continues. Fade out.

Fade in again on the same scene as CORINNE appears in the background. Something catches her attention and she runs forward, calling to ROLAND.

CORINNE : *Roland! There's some people!*

Camera tracks out as she runs towards us down a path between some trees. ROLAND comes down the bank at the side of the path and stoops to wash his face in a puddle. CORINNE walks towards the people she has seen.

CORINNE : *Hallo!*

ROLAND following her : *D'you come from here? Are you locals?*

We follow them as they come up to camera and, receiving no reply, halt and look off in the direction of the people.

CORINNE : *Are you deaf or what?*

ROLAND : *Are you blind or what?*

With them we look down the tree-lined track to a scene of pastoral tranquility. Sun filters through the emerald foliage and in the middle distance are EMILY BRONTE, in a straw hat and flounced dress, and TOM THUMB, wearing knickerbockers and a tam o'shanter. As they come towards us, TOM THUMB wanders from side to side of the track, inspecting the vegetation; we see that he has pieces of paper pinned to various parts of his jacket. EMILY is reading from a book.*

Resume on CORINNE and ROLAND staring at the scene in disbelief. They exchange glances and shrug.

Resume on the other couple. TOM THUMB and EMILY make their way slowly towards camera. He picks up a pebble and gives it to her while he looks at a note pinned to his sleeve and starts to declaim :

TOM THUMB : *Robbed in Los Angeles, the city where dreams are for*

---

* End of reel four.

sale, I realized that I was carefully keeping quiet about the theft, committed by an emigrant like myself . . .

CORINNE off : *Mademoiselle . . .*

TOM THUMB reading from his sleeve : *. . . and a reader of all my poems . . . as though I feared that this evil deed might be found out by . . . the animals, let us say.*

ROLAND off : *Mademoiselle . . .*

EMILY hands TOM THUMB back the pebble.

TOM THUMB : *Thank you, Miss Brontë.*

EMILY : *You're welcome, pet.*

CORINNE off : *Mademoiselle . . .*

EMILY : *Yes, what is it?*

EMILY goes off in the direction of CORINNE and ROLAND while TOM THUMB continues to wander to and fro, tossing the pebble in his hand.

CORINNE off : *We're sorry to bother you but . . .*

ROLAND off : *We'd like to know if we're on the right road for Oinville.*

ROLAND and CORINNE are back to camera beside a large wooden gate. EMILY wanders around in the background.

EMILY : *Are you seeking poetical or concrete information?*

ROLAND impatiently : *Is Oinville this way or that way?*

CORINNE : *That's all we want to know — this way or that way?*

Camera pans to include TOM THUMB, who stands tossing his pebble. The gate, which blocks the entrance to the track, has NO ENTRY written in white letters across the top, but there is no fence on either side of it.

EMILY walking round in a circle : *Physics does not yet exist . . . only individual physical sciences. Perhaps they're not yet physical, even.*

ROLAND who has come round the end of the gate : *This film's crap. We're always meeting nut-cases.*

CORINNE opening the gate and going through : *It's your own fault . . .*

Camera pans to show ROLAND sitting at the foot of a tree. CORINNE leans against the trunk behind him.

CORINNE : *There's nothing to stop you from leaving.*

ROLAND irritably : *Nag, nag, nag . . .*

Resume on EMILY and TOM THUMB in medium shot. She picks up another pebble from beside the track and starts walking round him again. He puts his pebble in his pocket. (Still on page 73.)

TOM THUMB looking at his wrist : *But perhaps fate knows everything*

56

and only pretends to get things wrong. Hesitantly, it gives one seven years of happiness, then, undecided, it takes two away . . . EMILY drops the second pebble into his palm. *Thanks Emily.*

EMILY : *You're welcome, pet.* She moves away from camera to pick up another pebble.

CORINNE off : *Mademoiselle, please . . .*

Pan as EMILY comes up and shows the pebble to ROLAND.

EMILY : *What's this?*

ROLAND off : *That? It's a pebble.*

TITLE blue letters :   DU COTE
                            DE CHEZ
                            LEWIS
                            CARROLL

Close-up of the pebble in EMILY's hand, brightly lit against the dark background.

EMILY off : *Poor pebble. Architecture, sculpture, mosaic, jewellery have ignored it . . . It dates back to the beginnings of the planet, sometimes it even comes from another star . . . and then it is warped in space and bears the scars of its terrible fall . . . It dates from before mankind, and then, when man came along, he did not incorporate it either into his art or his industry. He did not manufacture it, assigning to it a humble, luxurious or historical status. The pebble perpetuates nothing save its own memory.*

EMILY's face is seen in profile.

EMILY : *These words must not be misunderstood. Obviously minerals are neither independent nor sensitive. Which is precisely why it takes a lot to stir them — the temperature of a blow-torch, for example, or an electric arc, earthquakes, or volcanic eruptions, without forgetting the headlong progress of time . . .*

ROLAND is heard yelling at her angrily.

ROLAND off : *We want to know the way to Oinville. The-way-to-Oinville!*

She doesn't react.

A medium shot shows TOM THUMB by a tree-trunk in the foreground, tossing his pebble in the air. In the background ROLAND chases EMILY down the track, shaking her brutally and yelling at her.

ROLAND : *The-way-to-Oinville!*

57

Corinne chasing after her also : *Oin-ville, Oin-vi-lle, Oin-vi-lle, Oin-vi-lle!*

We follow them as Emily, quite unmoved, wanders across and picks up a piece of grass from the side of the track.

Roland shouting : *Oinville!*

Emily holding up the piece of grass : *And I want to know what this is.*

Roland snatches it from her and throws it over his shoulder.

Roland impatiently : *It's a bit of grass.*

Emily : *No, it's* poa nemoralis. She goes off.

Roland yelling : *Well, what about Oinville?*

Corinne impatiently : *Is it this way or that way?*

Tom Thumb appears, waving a branch above his head.

Emily reappearing : *And what's this?*

Corinne taking the branch : *Chestnut leaves.*

Emily : *No, they're* castanea sativa.

We follow Tom Thumb and Emily as they move away from the other two and Tom Thumb begins declaiming once more.

Tom Thumb reading from a note on his lapel : *On the morning of a new day* . . .

Roland and Corinne shouting and whistling off-screen : *Oh no! Save it for the Olympia! . . . Cut it out!*

Tom Thumb continuing unperturbed : *In the still grey dawn, vultures will take wing in despair, on faraway shores, flying noiselessly in the name of Order* . . . Emily hands him another pebble . . . *Thanks, Miss Brontë* . . . He goes off.

Emily : *You're welcome, pet.* She opens her book again.

Corinne off : *Mademoiselle, please, I beg you, we've been in an accident. Some people are expecting us* . . .

Emily : *And I beg you to help me. I absolutely must find the solution to this problem* . . .

Roland comes up to her and grabs at the book.

Roland : *Now what? . . .* Looking at the book : *Ah, shit!*

Medium close-up of the two of them by the tree. (Still on page 73.) Music as Emily starts reading from the book, while Roland wanders off in disgust in the background.

Emily reading : *One — a kitten which likes fish can be educated. Two — no kitten without a tail is ready to play with a gorilla. Three — kittens with whiskers always like fish. Four — no kitten which loves learning has green eyes. Five — no kitten with whiskers has a tail. So, what's the answer?*

ROLAND comes back towards her, hefting a chunk of rotten wood.

ROLAND : *No idea.*

We see EMILY facing camera. She glances at the others.

EMILY : *Now this one.*

CORINNE off : *Oh my God!*

EMILY reading : *One — no shark doubts the fact that it is well armed . . .*

CORINNE passes in front of camera, swiping at the book as she does so.

EMILY continuing unperturbed : *Two — a fish which cannot dance the minuet is only to be despised. Three — no fish can be quite sure of being well-armed unless it has three rows of teeth. Four — all fish, except for sharks, are kind to children. Five — no corpulent fish can dance the minuet. Six — a fish with three rows of teeth is by no means to be despised . . . Well, what's the answer?*

TOM THUMB off : *Miss Emily!*

EMILY impatiently to CORINNE : *What's the answer?*

CORINNE off : *I don't know.*

CORINNE appears and stands in front of the tree while EMILY goes off towards TOM THUMB.

TOM THUMB off : *Miss Emily! Miss Emily!*

TITLE blue letters :   THE FILM
                            DISTRIBUTORS
                            AGAINST POOR BB

TOM THUMB off : *Stop punishing petty crimes . . .*

ROLAND off : *You're beginning to get on my nerves. We're trying to be friendly, but you really take the cake . . .*

TOM THUMB simultaneously off :*. . . and crime will die out of its own accord.*

Medium shot : ROLAND is trying to shut up TOM THUMB, while EMILY swipes at him with her parasol. He grabs the stone she is holding in her hand, then rummages in TOM THUMB's pockets for the others.

TOM THUMB : *Think of that black night, of the cold, in this vale of tears and horror . . .*

ROLAND yelling : *Shut up!*

TOM THUMB : *. . . but hunt down the real thieves, the big ones . . .*

Roland : *Shaddup!*

Tom Thumb : *. . . start exterminating them today.*

Roland : *Shaddup!*

Tom Thumb shouting louder and louder, staring at his forearm : *From them comes the cold.*

Roland hurling a stone at him : *Belt up!*

Camera pans with Tom Thumb as he rushes off into the undergrowth, still declaiming at the top of his voice. Roland stands hurling stones after him.

Tom Thumb : *From them. From them comes the night.* Off : *It's because of them that the world is full of horror!*

Roland hurling a stone with all his might : *Cut it out!*

Emily stands in medium shot, pointing an accusing finger.

Emily : *Be he black or white, I demand the death of the crocodile, the everyday murderer.*

Roland rushes past, grabbing at her hand. Emily turns and points in the other direction. Music. Corinne rushes into shot and grabs her by the arm.

Corinne : *Cut it out. This isn't a novel, it's life. A film is life.*

She gives Emily a vicious push. Camera pans with Emily as she runs away.

Emily : *We must cover the flowers with flames, we must stroke their hair, we must teach them to read . . .*

Roland and Corinne rush after her and catch her.

Roland : *So you want to cover the flowers with flames, do you, so you want them covered in flames!*

Corinne holds Emily while he bends down and lights a match.

Emily : *Ow! Ow!*

High angle close-up : the bottom of her dress flares up.

Emily screaming off : *Ow! Ow! Ow!*

We see Roland and Corinne in medium close-up, looking down at the blazing Emily off-screen.

Corinne : *We are beastly, you know; we've no right to burn anyone, not even a philosopher.*

Roland lighting a cigarette : *Can't you see they're only imaginary characters?*

Corinne : *Why is she crying then?*

Roland : *I don't know. Come on.* He goes off.

Corinne stands for a moment looking down at the body.

CORINNE : *In fact we're not much more than that ourselves.*
She starts to follow ROLAND, turning back for a last look.
Seen from a high angle, EMILY is nothing but a blaze of orange flame. We hear the voice of TOM THUMB.
TOM THUMB : *I said to myself: what's the use of talking to them? They only buy knowledge to sell it again. All they're looking for is cheap knowledge they can sell for a high price. They are determined to win and they are not interested in anything which stands in the way of victory. They don't want to be oppressed, they want to oppress . . .*
As the flames die down a little, we see TOM THUMB sitting over the blaze in the background, declaiming in elegiac tones from a note pinned to his knee.
TOM THUMB : *. . . They don't want progress, they want to be first. They will submit to anyone so long as he promises that they can make the laws. What can one say to them, I wondered. Then I decided — this is what I shall say to them:*
Fade out.

TITLE blue and red letters :

ONE TUESDAY
IN THE 100
YEARS WAR

We look straight down at an earthworm, inching its way across a piece of muddy ground. The voices of ROLAND and CORINNE are heard off.
ROLAND off : *We don't know a thing.*
CORINNE off : *Yes, we are wholly ignorant about our own natures . . .*
ROLAND off : *As ignorant about ourselves as about this worm . . .*
CORINNE off : *We are ' enigmas ', both of us . . .*
ROLAND off : *And whoever denies it is the most ignorant of the ignorant.**
Medium shot of the couple, who are sitting in the middle of a field. CORINNE is now wearing a trilby hat and a green sweater. An aeroplane drones overhead.
ROLAND holding up the earthworm : *And whoever denies it is the most ignorant of the ignorant.* He drops the worm.
CORINNE, who has been gazing round at the scenery, suddenly

---

* End of reel five.

jumps up and runs off to the right.

CORINNE: *Hey look! That's a pair of trousers from Eddy's!*

ROLAND looking after her: *How many days has it been now, four?*

Seen from behind, CORINNE runs up to a couple of crashed cars at the roadside. An aged Renault has landed right on top of a green Mini. There are bodies lying around at various angles and blood is trickling down the door of the Renault.

CORINNE turning: *Yes, today's Thursday.*

She bends down and starts taking off the dead Renault driver's shoes. ROLAND appears and wanders across to the Mini.

ROLAND: *Your old man must have croaked by now. On Monday at the latest . . .* He takes a jacket out from inside the car and tries it on. *Your mother's going to give us hell. Christ, it's enough to make you sick. It's not fair.*

The jacket doesn't fit, so he throws it away. CORINNE is meanwhile pulling off the Renault driver's trousers.

CORINNE: *Bet you the old bitch will have altered the will! She won't want to share it now.*

Camera pans slightly as she brushes the trousers off and sits down at the roadside to put them on.

ROLAND: *We'll just have to torture her to make her change her mind. I remember when I was a lieutenant in Algeria they taught us a trick or two . . .*

CORINNE glancing up the road: *Look, isn't that a lorry coming?*

ROLAND runs to look, then he rushes back and drags her into the middle of the road.

ROLAND: *Quick, quick, get those trousers off. Take them off and lie in the middle of the road. Hurry up, for God's sake! Go on, raise your knees. Open them wide, you idiot!*

She does so as a large yellow lorry comes round the bend in the background.

Reverse shot: CORINNE lies in the middle of the road with her legs apart while ROLAND squats behind the door of the Renault. The lorry comes past and grinds to a halt, almost running down CORINNE, who jumps out of the way just in time and shouts up to the driver.

CORINNE: *Are you going towards Oinville?*

ROLAND coming round the back of the lorry: *Will he take us?*

He waits for CORINNE.

CORINNE joining him : *Yes, but we've got to help him with his concert because the guy who was with him has made off with a bird.*
They open the back of the lorry and climb in. Camera pans to show some farm buildings in the distance as it drives off up the road. Sound of a piano playing Mozart.

TITLE blue letters :   MUSICAL

TITLE blue letters :   ACTION

Resume on the lorry approaching the farm buildings. Fade out.

TITLE blue letters :   MUSICAL
ACTION

We are now inside the farmyard. As the piano continues to play, camera pans and tracks very slowly in a wide circle, past farm buildings and machinery, while lounging farm hands listen to the music . . . A man in gum boots and a trilby hat walks with the camera as we pass ROLAND leaning back against a pole and CORINNE squatting on the ground at his feet, both bored to tears . . . We lose the man as we pass the yellow lorry, parked to one side of the farmhouse, a large building with white shutters and walls covered in creeper . . . Then we move on past some barns and a trio of women standing in a line, listening. At that moment the pianist — GEGAUFF — breaks off and addresses his audience. As he does so, camera continues to pan, passing a yellow trailer hitched to a tractor.
GEGAUFF off : *Basically there are two sorts of music — the sort you listen to and the sort you don't. Quite obviously Mozart belonged to the category you listen to, especially when you think of the vast royalties he'd get now, poor man . . . The sort of music people don't listen to is so-called serious modern music. Let's face it, almost no one goes to hear it . . .* An aeroplane flies overhead, almost drowning his voice *. . . The real modern music, on the other hand, is basically an adaptation of Mozart's harmonies. You can hear a bit of Mozart when you listen to Dario Moreno, the Beatles, the Stones or what have you. It's all based on Mozart's harmonies, whereas so-called serious modern music tried to find others . . .*
A man comes out from behind a lorry, walks along it keeping pace with the camera and climbs into the cab.

63

GEGAUFF continuing off : . . . *The result being that it's probably the biggest flop in the whole history of art. Right, I'll go on with the sonata as this bores the hell out of you . . . No, actually it's better to start again . . .*

We finally reach a vast concert grand piano with the top open, parked in the middle of the farmyard, the words BECHSTEIN PIANOS in large white letters on the side. GEGAUFF sits at the keyboard, wearing a scarf, with a cigar butt clamped between his teeth, while a girl stands ready to turn over the pages of the music. There are a couple of radiant heaters working from gas cylinders just behind them. (Still on page 74.) As GEGAUFF continues to play, camera starts to move again; completing a full circle, we once more pass ROLAND and CORINNE yawning with boredom . . . the yellow lorry . . . the farmhouse . . .

GEGAUFF breaking off once more, off-screen : *It's incredibly graceful don't you agree? To think that when the poor man died he was just tossed into a pauper's grave like a dog. Sad, isn't it, when you think of the tenderness of his melodies . . . However, let us remember that the whole of Vienna — happily — came to his funeral. They all had to leave again because of a snowstorm, if you recall. They were a lot of ungrateful dogs . . .*

We follow a man and a girl walking away from the farmhouse. The girl (Anna Wiazemsky) speaks in the man's ear as the plane roars overhead again.

GEGAUFF to his assistant, off : *Where was I, sweetie? No, not there. There. You ought to know. Yes, here I was.*

He starts playing again and the tracking camera loses the man while the girl, wearing a green and blue sweater with horizontal stripes, comes up and leans against the end of the piano . . . We come to a halt by the pianist again; his assistant turns the page. Then camera starts to move back round the farmyard in the opposite direction . . . As we pass the farmhouse, the man in gum boots reappears for a moment, carrying a shovel over his shoulder . . . We finally halt by ROLAND, still leaning against his post, yawning wide enough to break his jaw. CORINNE, who has left him for a moment, reappears and sits down at his feet.

CORINNE : *Not bad . . .*

The music stops again.

GEGAUFF off : *Don't think that I play well — my playing's fucking*

awful. If you could have heard Schnabel before the war — incredible.
I studied under him, he's dead now . . . he was a real pianist . . .
Roland lights another cigarette. A farm hand in a red shirt is
leaning up against a barn in the background.
Gegauff off : *. . . I'm just a turd. I play more or less like a pig and*
I hope you'll excuse me for it. If only you'd heard him — marvellous
. . . The plane roars overhead *. . . An incredible tone, he had. Anyway*
he rarely tackled Mozart because he used to say that Mozart was too
easy for children and beginners and too difficult for virtuosos.
He starts playing again. Camera starts to move again as the man
with the gumboots and shovel walks past. As he reaches the piano,
Gegauff breaks off with an oath.
Gegauff : *Shit! This bastard of a cigar's making me play wrong notes*
. . . There!
He puts the cigar butt in an ashtray on the side of the piano,
then continues playing. Fade out on the music.

Title blue and red letters :
THE WEEK OF
4 THURSDAYS

We hear the engine of Gegauff's lorry.
Long shot : the lorry is parked by the roadside, an overturned car
in the background. Gegauff stops his engine, gets out of the cab
and goes round to the back of the lorry. He opens the doors and
points down the road.
Gegauff : *It's that way, straight on.*
Corinne and Roland jump out and shake hands with him.
Corinne : *Goodbye, and thank you.*
Roland : *Thanks.*
Gegauff gets back into his lorry and drives off.
Roland to Corinne : *It's your turn.*
He forces her to give him a piggy back. Music as she staggers
away past a field of sweet corn. Fade out.

Title blue letters : ONE FRIDAY
FAR FROM

Voices off : *Siamo gli attori italiani della coproduzione . . .*
Walking along a woodland track, Roland and Corinne pass a
trio of Italians, two of them seated on a log, the other standing

65

behind them with an umbrella — it is raining. They raise their hands in greeting.

CORINNE : *What are that lot doing?*

TITLE blue letters :

    ONE FRIDAY
    FAR FROM
    ROBINSON
    AND MANTES
    LA JOLIE

ITALIANS in chorus, off : *Siamo gli attori italiani della coproduzione.*

ROLAND off : *They're the Italian actors in the co-production.*

ONE ITALIAN off : *Siamo gli attori italiani della coproduzione.*

Cut to black.*

Fade in to a shot of a large lorry lying on its side in a ditch; its dead driver is hanging half out of the open door of his cab. It is pouring with rain, and the surface of the road which runs past in the foreground is glistening wet. Beyond the lorry, CORINNE staggers towards us with ROLAND on her back. She finally throws him off with a curse. ROLAND jumps over the ditch onto the road and walks along by the lorry while CORINNE disappears behind it.

ROLAND : *Hey, come on.*

Camera pans with him as he leans into the cab, takes the lorry driver's jacket and walks along the road putting it on.

ROLAND : *Are you coming?*

CORINNE reappears from behind the lorry and throws herself down on a grassy bank at the roadside.

CORINNE : *I've had enough.*

ROLAND sits down a little way away from her and starts wiping the mud off his shoes. We hear a car approaching. ROLAND gets up and flags it down. The car — a white Triumph Spitfire — comes to a halt beside him.

GIRL PASSENGER : *Are you in a film or are you for real?*

ROLAND walking round to the driver's side : *In a film.*

DRIVER : *In a film? Liars!* He accelerates off up the road.

CORINNE and ROLAND jumping up and down in fury : *Bastard! Bastard! Bastard!*

ROLAND walks towards CORINNE, who has jumped down into the

---

* End of reel six.

ditch at the roadside.

ROLAND : *Come on, we'll find the way in the end.*

CORINNE shaking her head : *No! I'm fed up. I just want to sleep. I'm going to croak.* She disappears into the ditch.

ROLAND : *Go ahead and croak then.*

He sits down at the roadside again and pulls out a cigarette as we hear the Spitfire accelerating away in the distance. Music as a TRAMP wearing a long overcoat with a haversack over his shoulder comes into view, plodding along the road. He has an unlit cigarette in his mouth. He passes ROLAND, who is just lighting his Gitane, halts, goes back and bends over him.

TRAMP : *Got a light?*

ROLAND putting out his match : *Nope.*

The TRAMP looks at him for a moment, then walks on a bit. He pauses, looking down into the ditch where CORINNE is lying, out of sight.

TRAMP to ROLAND : *There's a bird down here.*

ROLAND belligerently : *So what?*

TRAMP glancing down into the ditch again : *She your bird?*

ROLAND looks away but doesn't reply. The TRAMP climbs down into the ditch, disappearing from view.

CORINNE screaming off : *No, ouch, no, help! No, ouch! No, help!*

A plane drones overhead, and we hear another car approaching. ROLAND starts thumbing, then gets up as a large chauffeur-driven American saloon comes to a halt in front of him. He comes round to the driver's door and squats down with his back to us. ELLEN — a middle-aged, conservative-looking woman — leans out of the back.

ROLAND : *Are you going through Oinville?*

ELLEN : *Would you rather be fucked by Mao or Johnson?*

ROLAND : *By Johnson of course!*

ELLEN to the chauffeur : *Drive on, Jean.* To ROLAND : *Dirty fascist!* The chauffeur operates his electric window-winder and drives off up the road. Shoulders hunched against the rain, ROLAND goes wearily back to the roadside, cursing.

ROLAND : *Jesus Christ, Jesus Christ, Jesus Christ!* He sits down and yells after the departing car : *Jesus Christ!* He drags at his cigarette. Music as the TRAMP hauls himself out of the ditch and stands glancing at ROLAND while he buttons up his coat. Camera tracks

67

left along the road, losing first the TRAMP then ROLAND. Then it moves slowly back to ROLAND as CORINNE flops down beside him and sits there nursing a bruised shoulder. A pause, then CORINNE leaps up and flags down a passing Citroen.

CORINNE to the driver : *Are you going through Oinville?*

TITLE blue letters :

OO	/	OO	AND	/	FOOTIT AND
O O		CHOCOLATE			CHOCOLATE

MOTORIST off : *Who attacked first — Israel or Egypt?*

CORINNE off : *Those bastards the Egyptians . . .*

Resume on the scene. CORINNE gives a little jump to address ROLAND over the roof of the car.

CORINNE : *. . . Isn't that so, Roland?*

MOTORIST : *Ignorant fool!* He drives off.

CORINNE beckons wearily to ROLAND.

CORINNE : *Isn't that a road over there?*

She starts to walk on up the road, camera tracking slowly with her.

ROLAND coming up behind her : *Your turn.* He leaps on her back.

CORINNE counting the steps : *One, two three, four, five, six, seven, eight, nine, ten. Your turn.*

They change places.

ROLAND cheating and gabbling the numbers : *1 — 23456789 — 10.*

He tips her off his back. At that moment a lorry is heard approaching. They both stand in the middle of the road, waving. A yellow dustcart appears from the left and halts in front of them.

CORINNE to the DRIVER : *Are you going to Oinville?*

DRIVER : *Yes, climb in.*

They leap onto the lorry, helped by a couple of dustmen on the back. Camera pans right as the vehicle moves off up the road. Fade out.

Fade in to a shot of a thick green hedge. Camera cranes up to show CORINNE and ROLAND coming up a path carrying a pile of rubbish and a dustbin. CORINNE drops the rubbish all over the path and ROLAND kicks at it as he passes.

CORINNE : *Shit!*

Roland : *There's no need to spread it about . . . Come on.*

Camera pans as he comes up to the dustcart and heaves the dustbin onto the back of it. The two dustmen, a Negro and an Arab, are leaning against the side of the lorry having their lunch — they are both munching enormous sandwiches of French bread. Roland climbs onto the dustcart and empties out the dustbin. Then he sits down and searches around in the piles of rubbish for something to eat. He tries a bit of cauliflower stem but spits it out, then looks longingly at the Negro's sandwich.

Roland to the Negro : *Just a bite . . .*

The Negro takes a large bite himself, reflects, then hands Roland up a crumb. Roland swallows it and looks down again.

Roland : *A little bit more . . .*

Negro taking another vast bite and waving his sandwich : *That represented exactly the same proportion of my sandwich as the proportion of its overall budget which the U.S. gives to the Congo.*

Roland bored : *Yeah, yeah, sure . . .*

At that moment Corinne appears and tries to heave a couple of boxes of rubbish onto the dustcart.

Corinne : *Help me, Roland . . .*

Roland takes the boxes from her, throws them to the back of the cart and sits down again. Corinne approaches the Arab.

Corinne : *Monsieur, I'm hungry . . .*

The Arab pulls a piece off his sandwich, fends Corinne off as she reaches for it hungrily, then starts to eat it himself.

Arab in a nasal voice : *Kiss me!*

She kisses him gingerly on the cheek. He turns away and starts munching his sandwich again, then suddenly bawls at her :

Arab : *Kiss me!*

She kisses him on the mouth and he hands her the bit of sandwich; then, just as she is about to take a bite, he suddenly belts her.

Corinne indignantly : *Hey, knock it off, will you?*

Arab waving his sandwich : *I'm applying the law which the big oil companies apply to Algeria.*

Corinne walks between the Negro and the Arab, who are facing camera, and hands her bit of sandwich up to Roland.

Corinne : *What law?*

Roland getting up to take the sandwich : *What law?*

He helps Corinne up onto the cart.

Arab looking up at him : *The law of the kiss and the kick in the arse.*

Title blue letters :   WORLD

3

Corinne off : *Just because you're underprivileged you don't have to be mean!**

Close-up of the Arab, who is wearing a check tweed cap.

Arab : *My black brother will now express my views.*

He stares straight at camera, taking vast bites from his sandwich and munching, as the Negro declaims loudly. (Still on page 74.)

Negro off : *The optimism which reigns in Africa today is not an optimism inspired by the sight of the forces of nature at last proving beneficial to the Africans.* Music. *Nor is this optimism due to the fact that the erstwhile oppressor is now acting in a less inhuman and more benevolent fashion. Optimism in Africa is the direct outcome of revolutionary action by the African masses, whether political or military — and often both at the same time. Recently, a large section of humanity was shaken to the core by the emergence of an ideology — Nazism — which brought a resurgence of the most primitive methods of torture and genocide . . .*

The Arab gropes in his mouth with one finger, staring straight at camera. Then he swallows and takes another bite of his sandwich.

Negro continuing off : *Those nations which were most immediately threatened by Nazism formed an alliance and committed themselves not only to the liberation of their occupied territory but also to literally breaking the back of Nazism, to destroying the evil where it had first taken root . . .* The Arab swats at a fly *. . . to liquidating the regimes born of this ideology.*

Flashback to Joseph Balsamo forcing the Facel into a three-point turn as the Negro continues.

Negro off : *Well, the African peoples must recall that they too have been subjected to a form of Nazism, to a form of exploitation . . .*

Resume on the munching Arab.

Negro off : *. . . to a deliberately conducted process of physical and spiritual liquidation; they must concentrate specifically on the French,*

---

* End of reel seven.

English and South African manifestations of this evil, but they must
also be ready to confront this evil as such throughout the African con-
tinent . . . We, the African people, declare that for over a hundred
years the lives of two hundred million Africans have been held cheap
or denied, haunted continually by the spectre of death. We declare
that we must not trust in the good will of the imperialists but that we
must arm ourselves with strength and militancy . . .

The ARAB takes another bite, then picks his teeth.

NEGRO off : *. . . Africa will not be freed by the mechanical develop-*
ment of her natural resources — rather, it is the hands and brains of
her people which are setting in motion the dialectics of the continent's
liberation and which will bring this process to a successful conclusion.

Flashback to SAINT-JUST declaiming in the field with CORINNE
and ROLAND walking away behind him. The NEGRO's voice continues.

NEGRO off : *Given these conditions, we may indeed have cause for*
optimism.

Close-up of the NEGRO wearing a red shirt and a black donkey
jacket.

NEGRO : My Arab brother will now speak for me.

Now he starts to munch his sandwich, staring at camera, while
the ARAB declaims off-screen. (Still on page 75.)

ARAB off : *Now that the hour of liberation is here, you scrape the*
bottom of the barrel in the hope of finding non-violent men, pacifists
hardened to suffering who are prepared to forgive the wrongs done
them by others . . . This is not what I am seeking. I maintain that a
black man's freedom is as valuable as that of a white man. I maintain
that, in order to win his freedom, a black man is entitled to do what-
ever other men have had to do to win theirs. I maintain that neither
you nor I will ever win our freedom by non-violence, patience and
love . . .

The NEGRO looks from side to side.

ARAB off : *. . . We will never obtain our freedom until we can make*
the world realize that it is our right, yours and mine, to follow the
example of all those who have sacrificed their own lives and taken the
lives of other men in order to be free, that it is in our power to do this
and that we are ready to follow their example . . . We, the black
people, are at war with the United States and its friends. We cannot
actually go to war against them as we have no heavy guns, and even

71

if we had we would not be able to use them . . . In addition we are fewer in number; we have therefore chosen guerilla warfare as the only possible solution.

The NEGRO takes another bite . . .

ARAB off : *. . . It is an advantageous tactic for us and an easy one to apply — we work in the nation's strategic points, in the factories, the fields and the white men's homes . . .*

Flashback to the first accident on the way to Oinville. The motorcycle policeman beckons the queue of traffic past the crashed cars and bodies strewn on the verge.

ARAB off : *. . . We can easily destroy and commit acts of sabotage, often without firing a single shot. For example, we can destroy telephone wires, railway lines, airfields, electric and electronic installations . . .*

Resume on the NEGRO as he bites off another piece of his sandwich.

ARAB continuing off : *The life of every Western city depends on an electronic system; if it is paralysed, the city is paralysed also. That is how, city by city, we will bring the West to its knees— by ruining it economically. At the same time we will engage in bloodthirsty acts of sabotage; it is for this purpose that we are studying the techniques of modern guerilla warfare and are drawing inspiration from the example set by the Vietcong. Our black brothers who are fighting for white America in Vietnam are gaining precious lessons in modern guerilla warfare. When they come back among us, they will be useful not only as soldiers who are not afraid of death but also as teachers of guerilla methods . . .*

The music, which has continued throughout this sequence, swells up as the NEGRO takes another bite from his sandwich.

ARAB off : *. . . Of course, as far as acts of sabotage involving bloodshed are concerned, the main problem is that of weapons. But all the blacks have at least a rifle or a revolver in their homes, and Molotov cocktails are easy enough to make. In any case, we have the means of obtaining weapons. I will say no more, but we have the means.*

The NEGRO raises his sandwich to his mouth.

TITLE blue letters :

CID   /   THE OCCIDENT   /   DENT

We see ROLAND and CORINNE from below, squatting on the rub-

72

PIANOS
BECHSTEIN

bish on the back of the lorry, staring down at the two dustmen off-screen. (Still on page 75.) The NEGRO takes over.

NEGRO off : *To be civilized means to belong to a class society, to a reality full of contradictions in which the development of the means of production is necessarily bound up with the development of methods* . . .

Flashback to the traffic jam : angry motorists gather round the Facel, which has halted near a horse and cart.

NEGRO off : . . . *whereby one group of men exploits another* . . . *Slavery, serfdom, wage-slavery* . . .

Resume on ROLAND and CORINNE. ROLAND sighs and glances up at her.

NEGRO off : . . . *' are the three principal forms of servitude characteristic of the three great periods of human civilization.'* According to Engels, the development of the class system and of the relations between classes is exemplified in the history of the West, starting with the Greeks and ending up with industrialized capitalism.

ARAB off : *Private property, the monogamous family and the state* . . .

Flashback to the scene in the parking lot in front of the apartment block. GEORGES rushes across and fires his shotgun at the departing Facel.

ARAB continuing off : . . . *when these three elements are brought together within a given society, that society has evolved from barbarism to civilisation* . . .

Resume on CORINNE and ROLAND.

ARAB off : . . . *and from a classless society to a society of classes.*

They exchange glances.

NEGRO off : *Let us define these terms. According to Morgan, whom Engels used as a point of departure* . . .

Flashback to ROLAND and CORINNE walking along the road between the blazing cars.

NEGRO off : . . . *mankind progresses from an advanced state of savagery to a primitive state of barbarism when it moves from a clan society to a tribal one* . . .

Resume on the two of them sitting on the rubbish on top of the dustcart.

NEGRO off : . . . *Mankind moves on from a primitive state of barbarism to an intermediary one when society evolves from the tribe to a confederation of tribes; and it moves from the intermediary to the*

81

advanced barbarian state when society evolves from a confederation of tribes to a form of military democracy. Thus mankind, in its 'heroic' state, just before entering on the stage of civilisation — in other words class society — finds itself organized in a 'military democracy'.

Flashback to a continuation of the scene with JOSEPH BALSAMO. In the distance, the Facel drives away from his red coated figure, only to find its way blocked by the flock of sheep as they stream across the road.

ARAB off : *Thus Greece at the time of its heroes and Rome at the time of its so-called kings were in fact military democracies . . .*

Resume on ROLAND and CORINNE on the dustcart. They look half bored, half riveted by what is being said. The music swells up as the ARAB continues.

ARAB off : *. . . which were based on and had emerged from the gentes, phratries and tribes . . . Even though the new patrician nobility had already gained some ground, even though they were gradually being awarded an increasing number of privileges, none of this altered the basic way in which these societies were originally constituted.*

NEGRO off : *Thus Greek society evolved from a tribal system into a confederation of tribes, then into a military democracy . . .*

CORINNE takes the cigarette from ROLAND's lips, drags at it, then stares absently into space. ROLAND takes it back as the NEGRO continues.

NEGRO off : *. . . If we are to understand this evolution we must have a clear notion of the gentilitial organisation on which it is based . . . Engels, like Morgan, assumed that . . .*

Flashback to TOM THUMB declaiming over the charred remains of EMILY BRONTE.

NEGRO off : *. . . the American concept of the gens was the original one . . .*

Resume on ROLAND and CORINNE.

NEGRO off : *. . . and that the Greco-Roman form was merely an advanced derivation of it.*

ARAB off : *He assumed that the gens of the Iroquois and especially that of the Senecas was the purest form of this primitive gens . . .*

In a high angle shot, we see a girl dressed in red and yellow, with a hippy headband and a rifle over her shoulder. She walks past a couple of other hippy figures, who are seated on a grassy bank above a lake, jerking in time to an unheard rhythm.*

ARAB continuing off : *Moreover the Iroquois had evolved during the nineteenth century to the stage of organizing into tribal confederations . . .*

Resume on CORINNE and ROLAND.

ARAB off : *The study of the Iroquois pattern thus became fundamental to an understanding of the early history of the West. However, according to Marx and Engels, the Iroquois confederation was not the most advanced form of social organization attained by the American Indians.*

NEGRO off : *For instance, the great pre-Columbian civilizations (the Incas, the Mayas and the Aztecs) . . . Music . . . had reached the final stages of their independent history and were at the same stage of development as the Greeks right at the end of their heroic age, about to embark upon their history as a class society.***

Camera pans with the dustcart as it drives up a country lane and round a bend, the ARAB and the NEGRO standing on the running boards on either side. Suddenly, ROLAND stands up on the garbage at the back.

ROLAND shouting : *Hey, stop, stop, stop!* He bangs on the back of the cab. *Stop, stop!*

The lorry comes to a halt and he jumps down and helps CORINNE down from the back.

ROLAND to CORINNE : *Come on, quick. Hurry up!*

The lorry drives off into the distance and the couple start pelting towards camera.

CORINNE : *Hey, we're at Oinville! Now for a bath!*

ROLAND : *Me first!*

TITLE blue letters :   WEEKEND

Resume on the same shot of the two of them, camera panning as they run towards us.

ROLAND pulling CORINNE back : *Me first!*

TITLE blue letters :   WEEKEND

ROLAND off : *It's not our fault we weren't here when your father*

---

* This is a flash-forward to a later sequence.
** End of reel eight.

died . . .
Resume on the running couple.
ROLAND chasing after CORINNE : *No, no, me first!*

TITLE blue letters : WEEKEND

ROLAND off : *. . . and she had to do everything.*
Fade in to a shot of CORINNE sitting in the bath, pouring out bath essence from a plastic bottle. A striped bath towel and a half-length painting of a naked woman are hanging on the wall behind her. (Still on page 76.) She addresses ROLAND off-screen.
CORINNE : *What did she say exactly?*
ROLAND off : *That she'd changed her mind about splitting fifty-fifty.*
CORINNE banging down the bottle on the end of the bath : *All that for nothing, it's enough to make you puke.*
ROLAND off : *What's this book?*
CORINNE washing her arms : *Someone lent it to me.*
ROLAND starts to read aloud from the book.
ROLAND off : *Originally, the hippopotamus lived on the land, but he went to see the Lord of the animals and asked him for permission to live in the water.*
CORINNE inspecting her fingernails : *We won't let her get away with it.*
ROLAND reading off : *The Lord refused. 'Why?' asked the hippopotamus, annoyed. 'Because you are a monstrous beast,' replied the Lord . . .*
CORINNE emphatically : *I swear she won't get away with it.*
She picks up a comb from the side of the bath and starts flicking at her fringe with it.
ROLAND off : *. . . of the animals, 'and because you'd eat all the fish.' 'No,' said the hippopotamus, 'I swear on my honour that I wouldn't eat a single fish.'*
CORINNE runs the comb down her nose, then puts it down again at the side of the bath.
ROLAND off : *'Whoever would believe a hideous creature like you?' the Lord said impatiently.*
CORINNE : *She won't get away with it, Roland.*
She sits soaping herself mournfully as ROLAND continues to ignore her. He is cleaning his teeth while he reads from the book.
ROLAND off : *The hippopotamus thought this over. At last he said: 'Master, I'll make a deal with you. If you allow me to live in the*

water, every time I want to shit I'll spread the shit out with my tail so that you can see for yourself that there aren't any fish bones in it.' ... The Lord of the animals deemed that the offer was a reasonable one and the hippopotamus was given permission . . . He rinses his mouth and spits . . . *to spend his days in the water.*
CORINNE loudly, as he finishes: *She won't get away with it, Roland!*

TITLE blue letters: LIFE IN THE

CORINNE'S MOTHER calling off: *Corinne, Roland, hurry up!*
    Long shot of a sunlit street in Oinville with a church in the distance. The sounds of CORINNE soaping herself in the bath and ROLAND reading continue.
ROLAND off: *By day, the hippopotamus is a completely different creature. At least the night conceals his astonishing display of ugliness . . . his bulging eyes . . .*
CORINNE interrupting, off: *Listen Roland.*
ROLAND continuing without a pause, off: *. . . his gigantic mouth, his misshapen body, his absurdly short legs, and his grotesque tail . . .*
CORINNE louder, off: *Listen to me!*
ROLAND taking no notice, off: *Perhaps, from a hippopotamus's point of view, this represents the acme of beauty . . .*
CORINNE getting annoyed, off: *For God's sake listen to me!*

TITLE blue letters: SCENE FROM
                         LIFE IN THE
                         PROVINCES

ROLAND reading louder off: *. . . but I am not a hippopotamus . . .*
    Resume on the street scene.
ROLAND off: *I look upon him not only as . . .*
    Flash shot of a pop-art advertisement for Total petrol.
ROLAND off: *. . . the most ungainly beast . . .*
    Another street scene. A car passes in the foreground.
ROLAND off: *. . . of all . . .*

TITLE blue letters:

                                 SCENE FROM
LIFE IN THE   /   LIFE IN THE
                                 PROVINCES

CORINNE impatiently, off: *Listen to me, Roland!*

Resume on the first street scene.

ROLAND off : ... *but also as an infinite* ...

Shot of CORINNE sitting in the bath.

ROLAND off : ... *abyss* ... Iris out.

TITLE blue letters : A FILM FOUND
ON A SCRAP HEAP

ROLAND off : ... *of stupidity.*

TITLE blue letters : A FILM
ADRIFT
IN THE
COSMOS

CORINNE off : *Listen to me!*

TITLE blue letters : A FILM FOUND
ON A SCRAP HEAP

ROLAND off : *I would not* ...

TITLE blue letters : A FILM
ADRIFT
IN THE
COSMOS

ROLAND off : ... *have dwelt* ...

TITLE blue letters : A FILM FOUND
ON A SCRAP HEAP

ROLAND off : ... *at such length on the disgust* ...

Resume on the second street scene.

ROLAND off : ... *which this horrible creature inspires in me* ...

CORINNE shouting, off : *Listen to me, Roland!*

ROLAND off, taking no notice : ... *were it not for my conviction that the servile way in which he accepts collective life is the most abject side of his nature.*

A yellow post van passes in the foreground.

CORINNE off, in quieter tones : *Listen, Roland, we've got to do something* ...

ROLAND shouting, off : *Nag, nag, nag, nag, nag!*

86

TITLE blue letters : SCENE FROM
 LIFE IN THE
 PROVINCES

CORINNE off, to her MOTHER : *Where are you going?*
MOTHER off : *To get the rabbit from Monsieur Flaubert.*
ROLAND off : *Sixty-forty, Mother-in-law.*
As he finishes, fade in to a high angle shot of the MOTHER's garden in Oinville, with trees and shrubs and a broad expanse of grass. The MOTHER comes striding up the slope towards us, past some bushes, with ROLAND at her heels.
MOTHER : *Out of the question!*
ROLAND : *Seventy-thirty, Mother-in-law . . .*
MOTHER : *Out of the question!*
ROLAND : *Eighty-twenty!*
MOTHER : *No, it's out of the question!*
As they come into the foreground, camera starts to pan with them and we see that the MOTHER is holding a skinned rabbit. ROLAND, walking behind her with his hands behind his back, has a yellow scarf wound round his neck.
ROLAND : *Oh, come on, Mother-in-law, be reasonable. Ninety-ten!*
They go up some steps towards the house and we see CORINNE standing in the doorway in the background, wearing a white house-coat.
CORINNE protesting : *Hey, that won't do, we'd only get four million! It's out of the question!*
ROLAND suddenly takes off his long yellow scarf and leaps on the MOTHER from behind.
ROLAND : *Right, let's get her!*
He throws the scarf round her neck, then slings her to the ground, shouting to CORINNE who has momentarily disappeared.
ROLAND : *Get a move on, for Christ's sake!*
As the MOTHER goes down screaming, CORINNE rushes out of the door, brandishing a large kitchen knife. She runs across the patio and stabs the knife repeatedly into her MOTHER's back.
We look down at the skinned rabbit lying on the gravel. As the MOTHER screams again and again off-screen, her blood pumps out onto the ground just by the rabbit's head. (Still on page 77.)
High angle close-up of the rabbit's head, the blood pumping out

beside it. The MOTHER continues to scream like an animal with its throat cut while ROLAND and CORINNE converse, off.

ROLAND off : *What'll we do?*

CORINNE off : *There's the Doctor Petiot method . . .*

ROLAND off : *No, the neighbours would see the smoke!*

CORINNE : *Well, then, what about the method used by Doctor Tar and Professor Feather?*

ROLAND off : *No, no . . .*

More crimson blood spurts out, completely covering the head of the skinned rabbit. The screaming dies away and a dog howls off-screen.

CORINNE off : *I know, let's shove her in the boot of the DS.*

ROLAND off : *And we'll find an accident on the motorway on the way home.*

CORINNE off : *We'll fix it to look as though the DS had been involved in an accident . . .*

ROLAND off : *And set the whole lot on fire with some petrol.*

CORINNE off : *Fantastic!*

ROLAND off : *It's the perfect crime!*

CORINNE off : *We'll live happily ever after.*

ROLAND and CORINNE together : *With the fifty million!*

CORINNE tenderly off : *I love you.*

ROLAND off : *Me too . . .*

The dog howls mournfully in the distance.

Long shot of a sign-post on the road leading into Oinville. A lorry moves past, going into the village, and then a yellow Citroen DS with CORINNE and ROLAND inside comes towards us in the opposite direction. Suddenly there is the loud droning of an aircraft accompanied by distorted sounds of car horns.

The sound continues as we see a yellow aeroplane which has crashed among some trees. A brightly coloured parachute dangles from the branches and a red car is upended against the fuselage, while the yellow DS lies on top of the pile of wreckage in the background. Fade out.

Fade in again to the same scene. The noise continues.

CORINNE : *There you are, I've put petrol over everything.*

She runs round the front of the plane while ROLAND jumps down from the DS in the background.

ROLAND : *Watch out, it's going to go up.*

They race across in front of the aircraft and ROLAND tosses a burning torch at the wreckage as he passes. Another aircraft continues to drone somewhere overhead. Loud music.

In a reverse angle long shot, the couple run towards us while the wrecked plane catches fire in the background. ROLAND suddenly turns and makes for some woods, over on the right.

CORINNE chasing after him : *Wait for me, you bastard!*

ROLAND over his shoulder : *Bastard yourself!*

The wreckage bursts into flames, sending out clouds of black smoke. Fade out as the music comes to a climax.

Fade in. A YOUNG MAN with a scanty beard, wearing a piped blazer with a buttonhole, is seen standing by a tree, dragging at a cigarette.

ROLAND off : *Is this the road to Versailles?*

Instead of replying, the YOUNG MAN pulls a novelty postcard out of his pocket, with a picture of a bird on it and a squeaker. He holds the card up in front of his face, squeaking it and looking off to the left.

YOUNG MAN : *Tweet tweet . . .*

TITLE blue and red letters :

F L   /   F L   /   F L

S   S   O

YOUNG MAN off : *Tweet tweet, tweet tweet.*

The music starts again as camera tracks with a figure dressed in hippy clothes, dashing through the undergrowth. He stops in a patch of sunshine, signals to someone, then dashes away into the trees. Camera tracks on over the tops of some bushes, then pans left to show ROLAND walking away from us down a track towards a main road in the distance . . . Suddenly there is furious shouting. We follow ROLAND as he turns and hurries across to where a large French family is having a picnic at the side of the track. Their car, an old Ford, is parked a little way away. They are all shouting at CORINNE who is trying to grab some food from them. ROLAND joins in, grabs a bottle of wine and swigs from it. Suddenly there is a shot and a puff of smoke drifts across the screen. They all stop shouting and look round in bewilderment as the YOUNG MAN seen earlier, accompanied by a girl with a sub-machine-gun dashes out from the trees in the background. At the same time another figure with a sub-machine-gun, wearing boots and a hippy headband, runs past camera and circles round the group. The girl— ISABELLE — takes charge and starts shouting orders to the others.

ISABELLE : *Quiet! On your feet! . . . Yves, the car!* The figure with the headband goes off to the right. *Claude, the food! . . . Stand up!*
One of the picnickers — LOUIS — a bearded, middle-aged man in shirt-sleeves and a trilby hat, moves forwards to protest as CLAUDE (the bearded young man) starts gathering up their provisions in a basket.

LOUIS : *What's going on?*

CLAUDE : *Shaddup you old fart!*
There is confused shouting as all the picnickers protest.

ISABELLE pointing at one of them, a middle aged woman : *The ugly one, down!*
YVES runs back to the group and picks up a bottle of brandy. We pan with him as he runs back to the car, opens the boot, then breaks the bottle and pours the alcohol over the petrol tank.

ISABELLE pointing to the woman's husband and their child : *The fat one, down! The kid, down!* She indicates a girl who is with ROLAND and CORINNE off-screen. *The bird and the other two over there, to one side.* Pointing to LOUIS, who is also off-screen : *The old one, down!*
The middle-aged woman pulls her husband down as he protests at what YVES is doing to the car.

CLAUDE off : *Belt up!*

ISABELLE shouting : *Quiet!*

LOUIS protesting off : *Hey, just what the hell is all this?*

ISABELLE : *Shut up!*

LOUIS off : *Shit, you've got a nerve!*

ISABELLE waving her sub-machine-gun at them : *Hey, everybody quiet!* She turns towards the car. *Hurry up, Yves.*
Camera pans slightly towards the left as YVES runs across to ISABELLE, hands her a box of matches and takes her sub-machine-gun. We then follow ISABELLE as she goes over to the car.

HUSBAND, waving his handkerchief : *He's setting fire to it!*
He begins to protest wildly as he realises what is about to happen.

YVES going off to the left : *Lie down!*
The HUSBAND starts to his feet as ISABELLE lights a torch and

flings it into the car.

YVES off : *Lie down!*

The car goes up with a roar. Camera pans left as ISABELLE comes back to the group.

ISABELLE pushing the HUSBAND and the little girl : *Lie down! The old guy, lie down!*

She comes across to LOUIS and hauls him to his feet.

LOUIS stumbling along ahead of her : *Wait for me, Mademoiselle!*

WOMAN protesting : *What do you want?*

Camera pans away from the WOMAN to hold on YVES as ISABELLE pushes LOUIS off to the left.

LOUIS shouting and waving at the car : *Christ's it's going up! Look at it burning!*

With a burst from his sub-machine-gun, YVES executes the remaining picnickers — the WOMAN, her HUSBAND and the little girl, all off-screen; then he turns and rushes after his companions as they haul the others away up a track into the trees.

ISABELLE shouting : *Get a move on!*

LOUIS in his thick accent, protesting : *We aren't in a hurry are we?*

ISABELLE pushing them on : *Will you get a move on, for Chrissake!*

GIRL : *Where're we going?*

Loud music. Camera tracks slowly after the group as they move on up the track.

YVES : Come on.

Fade out.

Sounds of running water. In a very high angle shot we see the group passing across a waterfall in single file. CLAUDE comes first, followed by the GIRL, who is wearing a red sweater, and LOUIS.

YVES in the background : *Get a move on!*

He urges them on with a shot from his gun, which echoes over the noise of the waterfall.

LOUIS stopping and turning round to gaze at the scenery : *Isn't it nice round here!*

ISABELLE shouting : *Quiet!*

CORINNE comes next, carrying the basket of provisions on her head.

CORINNE : *Listen, we've got money I tell you!*

YVES walking behind her, his gun slung over his shoulder : *Quiet!*

They pass by, then after a moment ROLAND comes into view,

staggering along in front of ISABELLE. She has now taken off the battledress she was wearing before to reveal a bright red PVC jacket.

ROLAND : *Now listen here . . .*

ISABELLE : *Come on, move!*

ROLAND : *Listen to me a moment!*

As he comes across the waterfall, ROLAND slips and falls flat on his face.

ROLAND struggling out of the water : *Are you a bunch of morons or what? We've got fifty millions in the bank, I tell you!*

ISABELLE waving him on : *Get a move on. Hurry!*

ROLAND looking up at her desperately : *Come with us and we'll give you half.*

ISABELLE mirthless : *Move, I said, move!*

Camera pans right as he hauls himself out of the water and on up the track, ISABELLE following. He has obviously injured his leg and is crawling along, dragging it behind him. They disappear into the greenery.*

The sound of running water is replaced by that of someone beating out a rock rhythm on a set of drums, as we cut to a high angle shot of the party advancing through a wood where the sunlight filters spasmodically through the trees. Camera pans right as CLAUDE, leading the party, strides past a character in a red shirt squatting on a pile of old tyres. He stops and hands him a book which he has been carrying under his arm.

RED SHIRT : *You found it, then?*

He takes the book and opens it as the rest of the party file past behind him. A figure in a striped jersey and a butcher's apron appears in the foreground and hails LOUIS.

GERALD going towards LOUIS : *Louis!*

LOUIS hailing him heartily : *What are you doing here, Gerald?*

YVES going off on the right : *Belt up!*

A VOICE off : *Valerie!*

The GIRL in the red sweater stands uncertainly in the centre of shot while CORINNE comes up beside LOUIS on the left, puts down the basket of provisions and flops to her knees.

VALERIE shouting off : *Who is it?*

---

* End of reel nine.

GERALD picking up the basket : *It's a pal of mine.*

LOUIS : ... *Yes, we fought together in Ethiopia.*

GERALD taking him by the arm : *Come over here.*

As the drumming continues, GERALD and LOUIS go off on the right while VALERIE, a tall girl wearing a pink dress and a bush-ranger's hat, walks towards the two women. She jerks CORINNE'S head up to look at her face, then walks round the GIRL in the red sweater, prodding her as though she was a piece of livestock. Meanwhile, ROLAND comes up from the left. VALERIE gives him a push in the back and he falls flat on his face. Camera tracks to the right, revealing KALFON, the revolutionaries' leader. Wearing an old-fashioned military uniform, he is seated pounding away at a set of drums on the edge of a clearing in the trees. He breaks off and looks up as VALERIE appears, shoving ROLAND and CORINNE in front of her.

KALFON : *What have we got?*

VALERIE : *One average male, one average female, one young female ...*

KALFON : *Let's have a look.*

He starts bashing the drums again while the other three move past in the background and halt a little way away. At the same time, YVES comes striding across from the opposite direction, his sub-machine-gun slung over his shoulder. KALFON gets up and hands him the drumsticks in exchange for the gun. YVES sits down and starts drumming away in his turn while KALFON goes up to the trio in the background. KALFON circles round, inspecting ROLAND and CORINNE while ISABELLE pushes the GIRL in red towards them from the left.

KALFON pointing to the GIRL : *That one'll do for Ernest. Right, make the others sit down.*

VALERIE pushes ROLAND and CORINNE to the ground. We follow ISABELLE as she shoves the GIRL towards the camp kitchen in foreground. ERNEST, the chef, is standing at his kitchen range with his back to us, cutting something up with an enormous butcher's knife. He is wearing a long white overall and butcher's cap liberally splashed with blood. ISABELLE throws the GIRL down at his feet and taps him on the shoulder.

ISABELLE : If you like, you can fuck her before you eat her.

ERNEST wipes his three-foot-long knife on his overall and turns

93

towards the girl. Camera pans with Isabelle as she walks away, revealing Yves sitting at the drums in the background. Fade out.

Title red, white and blue letters (crossed out with a large white cross) :
> LIBER
> ATION
> FRONT
> OF SEINE
> ET OISE

The noise of the drumming stops and Claude's voice is heard off-screen.

Claude off : *Battleship Potemkin calling The Searchers . . .*

A slightly high angle shot shows Claude squatting by a short-wave radio, leafing through a book in front of him as he talks into the microphone. Simultaneously, a girl wearing a hippy headband and carrying a rifle pours out a glass of wine for him, then goes off to the right.

Claude continuing : . . . *Over. Calling The Searchers.*

Voice on the radio, replying : . . . *The Searchers. I can hear you, Battleship Potemkin . . .*

As the radio continues off, we cut to the camp larder in another part of the woods. Several bodies of human beings or animals are lying at the foot of a tree.* The one in the foreground is recognisably a half-naked man, and another hippy girl is trussing him up and tying him to the tree with a chain.

Voice on the radio, off : *The Searchers speaking . . . Over. Go ahead Battleship Potemkin.*

An aeroplane flies overhead. The girl finishes her task and goes off as we hear the voice of Louis.

Louis in an exaggerated drawl, off : *It was in 1964. We were under the Trocadero bridge. It was hellish cold, d'you remember? It was the famous winter of '64 . . .*

As he continues, the blood-soaked chef appears, carrying his knife; he is accompanied by another girl wearing a red suede outfit with fringes and carrying the basket of provisions seen earlier. They stand over the bodies. Ernest starts taking eggs out of the

---

* The bodies would in fact appear to be those of Corinne and Roland, though as we see later, they both meet a different fate.

94

basket, breaking them ceremoniously with his knife and dropping them onto the pile of flesh. We hear music, which gets louder and louder, almost drowning Louis's words.

Louis off : . . . *And Alphonsine was so cold that she'd taken my prick in her hands to warm them. There she was, wanking me; it was so cold everything was frozen. And Alphonsine was saying: Wow, Louis, what a big prick you've got!* . . .

The music stops as Ernest finishes his task and comes towards camera, prodding the man's body with his knife as he passes.

Louis off : *And I said to her: That's not my prick, you idiot* . . .

Title blue letters :   TOTEM
                    AND   /
                    TABOO   TABOO

Louis off : . . . *it's just me shitting!*

A Voice off : *Come on* . . .

Laughter with electronic echo effect as we see a Hippy in a long pink Davey Crockett style head-dress prodding the Girl in the red sweater with the bayonet of his rifle.

Title blue letters :   TOTEM   TOTEM
                    /   AND
                       TABOO

The laughter continues over.

Resume on the Hippy and the Girl.

Hippy curtly : . . . *Sweater!* He signals to someone with his rifle. *Come on* . . .

The drumming starts again. He prods at the Girl's skirt with his bayonet.

Hippy : . . . *Skirt! Get a move on!* . . . *On your knees!* She kneels down. *Bra!* . . . *Pants!* . . .

She takes them off as the girl in red suede appears, carrying the basket of eggs.

Hippy : *Right, she's ready.* He goes off.

The drumbeats get louder and Red Suede starts frugging wildly to the rhythm, tossing a couple of eggs in the air. Ernest appears in his blood-soaked overalls, brandishing his three-foot butcher's knife.

Ernest shouting : *Lie down, you!*

95

The GIRL sinks to the ground.

TITLE blue letters :   TOTEM   TOTEM
                              /   AND
                                      TABOO

Resume on the scene. ERNEST is now kneeling over the GIRL, only the top half of his body visible, holding his knife up like a sword. Still frugging, RED SUEDE hands him an egg. A whistle blows off-screen.

TITLE blue letters :   TOTEM
                                     AND
                                     TABOO

In a low angle shot, RED SUEDE forces the victim's naked legs apart while ERNEST kneels in the background, an egg in one hand, the knife raised in the other. He cracks the egg with the knife, hands the latter to RED SUEDE, then drops the contents of the shell between the naked legs. The drumming gets louder and louder as RED SUEDE hands him another egg and he repeats the operation.

ERNEST : *The fish!*

RED SUEDE sticks the knife in the ground and produces a large, live fish from the basket. She hands it to ERNEST, who feeds it slowly and ceremoniously between the victim's thighs. Silence.

TITLE blue letters :

    GUST   /   A GUST   /

    AUGUST   /   AUGUST LIGHT

A motorbike is heard approaching.

Long shot of the motorbike approaching along the road by the wood. The rider signals to someone in the trees as he sweeps past and camera pans to show the party of revolutionaries and their victims making their way through the undergrowth. The revolutionaries signal to one another in whistles as they go. Hold as the motorcycle roars away and the revolutionaries squat down, forcing their prisoners to do likewise. KALFON and ROLAND are seen in the foreground. Behind them another hippy levels his rifle at CORINNE's head while ERNEST squats at the back of the shot, tap-

ping his knife on the ground. There is a long silence. ROLAND
looks round nervously, a Gitane hanging from his lips. Then
KALFON gets up, looking off to the left.

KALFON : *They're going* . . . He looks round at the others . . . *We'll
give them thirty seconds.*

He squats down again and they wait. Suddenly, ROLAND makes a
bolt for it, disappearing from view. A girl beside KALFON gets up
and levels her rifle after him, but KALFON stops her, pulls out a
catapult and lets fly. There is a terrible cry from ROLAND off-
screen.

ROLAND off : *Aaaaaaaaahhhhhhhhhh!*

KALFON turning to the chef : *Get him, Ernest.*

ERNEST hurries off while CORINNE tries to get to her feet.
Seen in medium close-up the girl with the rifle, JULIET,* forces
CORINNE to the ground again. The latter is now wearing a blood-
stained piece of cloth tied round her head like the hippies' head-
bands. Music. We hear ROLAND's death-rattle off-screen.

KALFON off : *Quickly now!*

JULIET taps CORINNE on the back of the neck with her rifle. She
jumps.

JULIET : *Get moving.*

TITLE red letters :

    M OR   /   T M OR   /   THERMIDOR**

ROLAND's death-rattle continues off :
A high angle shot shows ROLAND lying on his back on the ground
with blood oozing from his head. There is also blood all over his
shirt, but we cannot see further down than his chest. (Still on
page 77.)

ROLAND : *Aaaaaaarrrrrrgggggghhhhh!*

JULIET's feet pass by, followed by those of CORINNE.

CORINNE off : *Why have you opened his stomach?*

ERNEST off : *Because that's the best bit.*

CORINNE's feet pause by ROLAND's body.

---

* It is the same Juliet who appeared in the accident near the beginning of the
film.
** The 11th month in the Republican calendar instituted at the time of the
French Revolution (20th July to 18th August).

CORINNE off : *How horrible!*

KALFON'S feet stop just beside hers.

KALFON off : *We can only overcome the horror of the bourgeoisie by even more horror. Come on, get moving.*

He kicks her on the ankle and they walk off. Another pair of legs, clad in red stockings, follows them past. The music continues. Camera cranes up to show them crossing a stream in single file in the background. A policeman suddenly stands up from behind a bush on the other side of the stream and fires at the party. The girl in red stockings, who is last in the line, fires back and he falls.

TITLE blue and red letters :

		SEPTEMBER
MASSACRE	/	MASSACRE

Another shot is fired.

In a high angle medium shot two men are seen standing over a pig. One of them stuns it with a sledgehammer and it lies on the ground, its legs kicking. While the second man holds it still, the first one puts down the sledgehammer and cuts its throat with a knife. The blood gushes out.

TITLE blue and red letters :

		SEPTEMBER
MASSACRE	/	MASSACRE

JULIET off : *Get a move on!*

Another high angle shot. JULIET stands pointing her rifle at the first butcher as he squats on the ground, tearing the heart out of a goose which struggles violently. Another girl walks past in the background.

TITLE red letters :   PLUVIÔSE*

In a high angle long shot we look out over a calm lake across which a boat with three figures in it is rowing slowly towards us. Camera cranes down to show a girl sitting on the bank in the foreground, reading a book. The boat pulls in to the shore behind her and KALFON gets out, wearing his military tunic, a brace of dead rabbits in one hand and a couple of geese in the other.

---

* The fifth month in the Republican calendar (20th-22nd January to 19th-21st February).

98

Boatman shouting in the background : *What about my money!*
Kalfon pauses by the girl and looks down at her.
Kalfon : *Everything O.K., Mademoiselle Gide?*
Mademoiselle Gide looking up : *Fine thanks.*
Kalfon walks off to the left and Isabelle comes up the bank after him, carrying another rabbit and one of the drums from the drum kit.
Music over a general shot of the revolutionaries' camp. Valerie is seen on the left with another girl who is now wearing the bushranger's hat.
Valerie : *Come and look.* She leads her off to the right.
In the background, a naked girl stands with her hands tied to a tree while Claude paints her body. Louis stands watching a little way away.
Louis : *A bit of black would be nice too. And a bit of orange.**
A high angle shot shows the revolutionaries' field kitchen. In the foreground lie the dead pig and the mutilated goose, still flapping its wings in its death throes, while Ernest stands beyond them in his blood-soaked overalls, clattering his pots and pans on the range. Juliet watches him for a moment, then goes off, her gun over her shoulder. We hear the voice of the radio operator off-screen.
Claude off : *Johnny Guitar calling Gosta Berling . . .*
Clouds of steam arise as a pot hisses on the stove.
We now see Claude talking into the field radio, leafing through a book on his knees. In the foreground is a small motor scooter propped against a tree; the calm waters of the lake stretch away in the background.
Claude : *Johnny Guitar calling Gosta Berling . . . Can you hear me, Gosta Berling? Johnny Guitar calling Gosta Berling. Can you hear me?*
Voice on the radio, replying : *Gosta Berling speaking. I can hear you, Johnny Guitar. Over. Gosta Berling speaking . . .*

Title blue and red letters :

OCTOBER
LANGUAGE   /   LANGUAGE

Voice on the radio, off : *. . . I can hear you, Johnny Guitar. Over!*

---

* End of reel ten.

99

Camera tracks with Isabelle in her bright red PVC jacket and dark glasses as she walks through the undergrowth, gun in hand. Suddenly we hear Kalfon's voice declaiming loudly.

Kalfon off : *It is my intention . . .*

Drumbeats.

Title blue and red letters :

OCTOBER

LANGUAGE   /   LANGUAGE

The drumming continues off.

Resume on Isabelle stalking through the emerald green trees, camera tracking with her.

Kalfon declaiming off : *. . . to recite unemotionally and in a loud voice the cold and solemn lines you are about to hear. Listen carefully to their message and prepare to defend yourselves against the painful, scarring impression they will doubtless make upon your troubled imaginations. Do not assume that I am about to die, for old age has not yet left its stamp upon my brow. Therefore avoid any comparison between me and the dying swan, and look upon me only as a monster whose face you cannot see, thank God, although it is less hideous than its soul . . . Nevertheless, I am no criminal . . . Enough said . . .*

The tracking shot continues. Juliet has now appeared, stalking along with her gun, wearing a red jacket and yellow pants. Camera starts to move with her as she walks along the edge of the lake, losing Isabelle who goes off into the trees in the background.

Kalfon off : *Ancient Sea . . . On first sight of you, a breath as full of sadness as the soft murmur of the wind blows through the soul, leaving it deeply disturbed and marked for ever. Thus those who love you never fail to be reminded, sometimes unawares, of man's rude beginnings when he first learned the pain which has never left him since. Ancient Sea, I greet you . . .*

The drumming gets louder and faster and the camera tracks faster with Juliet as she walks along by the lake. We pass Kalfon, seated with his back to us, drumming away as he declaims . . . (Production still on page 78.)

Kalfon : *I suppose that man only believes in his own beauty out of vanity, but in fact suspects that he is not truly beautiful. Otherwise, why would he look with such contempt upon the faces of others made*

100

in his image?

. . . Then LOUIS, leaning up against a tree, holding a rifle.

KALFON off, still drumming away : *Ancient Sea, I greet you . . . Often, Ancient Sea, I have asked myself which is easier . . .*

We hold on a couple of hippy figures — CORINNE and VALERIE — squatting on the bank above the lake, nodding and jerking in time to the rhythm.

KALFON off : *. . . to fathom the depth of the ocean or the depth of the human heart. Allow me to say that, in spite of the ocean's depth, the depth of the human heart is on another scale altogether. Psychology still has a long way to go.*

As KALFON continues, JULIET, who has circled round the hippy figures, reappears in the foreground and walks past to the left.*

KALFON off : *Ancient Sea, I greet you! Ancient Sea, from your sombre depths you unfurl your matchless waves across the entire sublime breadth of your surface, calmly conscious of your eternal strength. Your moral grandeur reflects infinity, it is as vast as a philosopher's speculations, as the love of a woman, as the divine beauty of a bird . . .*

We begin to track back in the opposite direction again.

KALFON off : *Tell me, Ancient Sea, will you be my brother?*

We pass LOUIS again . . .

KALFON off : *I do not know what is your secret destiny, though all that concerns you is of interest to me. Tell me, therefore, if you house the Prince of Darkness. Tell me . . . tell me, O Sea. You must tell me, for I will rejoice to hear that hell is so close to mankind . . .*

. . . Then hold on KALFON in back view, drumming furiously.

KALFON : *Therefore, just once more, I wish to greet you and bid you farewell . . . Ancient Sea, I cannot go on, for I feel the moment has come to return to the harsh land of men . . .*

Camera cranes up slowly, losing KALFON, to show the broad luminous expanse of the lake stretching out beneath us.

KALFON off : *Let us take courage! Let us make a supreme effort and, conscious of our duty, fulfil our destiny on this earth . . . Ancient Sea, I greet you!*

The drumming stops. Fade out.

The scene changes to a farmyard. We are looking up a track to-

---

* It was this scene which we saw earlier in the episode on the dustcart.

wards a barn in the background. On the left is a low-built brick building, which is being covered by a figure squatting by the track with a sub-machine-gun. Further up the slope, CORINNE lies beside a pile of gravel. There are farmyard noises — the clucking of chickens etc. Then ISABELLE is heard shouting.

ISABELLE off : *O.K.!*

KALFON whistles and suddenly pops up from behind the bank of gravel in the centre of the shot.

KALFON shouting : *Right!*

He stands on the bank and waves to ISABELLE, then steps down onto the track and gives CORINNE a kick. She gets up and he hustles her towards camera, which pans to show ISABELLE coming towards them from some farm buildings in the background.

CORINNE turning to protest : *Please . . .*

KALFON : *Shut up!*

He pushes her on down the track, brandishing a pistol. ISABELLE follows in back view, covering them with a rifle, as they halt near some haystacks and look towards a couple of figures in the distance. A man with a shotgun shoves VALERIE up the track towards them; an exchange of hostages is about to take place. They draw level and halt, then KALFON suddenly shoves CORINNE across to the other man while VALERIE flies into his arms. Camera pans as they run up the track towards us, arm in arm, with ISABELLE following behind.

CORINNE shouting after them : *Don't leave me behind, I want to come with you!*

KALFON : *Too late! . . .*

As they run past the brick building there is a shot and a puff of smoke from its window.

KALFON : *Isabelle! . . .*

The man covering the building returns the fire with a burst from his sub-machine-gun, then he gets up and runs off after the others while ISABELLE comes up and trains her rifle on the window. A figure runs out of the back of the building and ISABELLE gives chase. They exchange shots and she falls, hit, while the man climbs up a bank in the background.

ISABELLE calling to the others : *Don't wait for me! Goodbye Valerie!*

VALERIE off : *Goodbye Isabelle!*

Suddenly the man with the shotgun — wearing gumboots and a

trilby hat — runs in from the left and fires after the fleeing revolutionaries. There is a scream off.

TITLE blue letters :   ARIZONA
                           JULES

Resume on the man. He fires again as CORINNE runs past, screaming hysterically, her hands over her ears.

TITLE blue letters :   ARIZONA
                           JULES

Long shot of the farmyard, a crashed car in the foreground. KALFON and VALERIE rush towards us and take cover behind the car, pursued by the man firing his shotgun. (Production still on page 78.) The character with the sub-machine-gun returns his fire from the corner of a building in the foreground and he runs for cover, while CORINNE disappears behind a barn. More shots are exchanged, then camera pans with KALFON and VALERIE as they run round the corner towards the right. At that moment a shot from the man who killed ISABELLE, somewhere among the farm buildings, catches VALERIE and she staggers. KALFON rushes to her and gathers her up in his arms.

We see VALERIE in close-up, blood running down her face from a wound in the temple, her head cradled in KALFON's arms. She starts to sing in a soft, girlish voice. (Still on page 79.)

VALERIE :

> *I want so much for you to realize,*
> *You whom I shall have to leave tonight,*
> *That though one may be suffering agonies,*
> *Yet still to others all may seem all right . . .*

A pause, then she continues.

> *With a broken heart one still can smile,*
> *Apparently indifferent,*
> *When the last word has to be written,*
> *In a novel which comes to a . . . bad end.*

She says the last two words in a whisper, then her head drops forward. She is dead.

TITLE blue letters :   DISCONTINUITY

Resume on her head, dropped onto KALFON's arm; her blood is

trickling onto his hand.

TITLE blue letters : DISCONTINUITY

Back to VALERIE.

TITLE blue letters : DISCONTINUITY

A high angle medium shot shows KALFON in back view, cradling VALERIE in his arms. There is more shooting, off, as he gives her a last farewell kiss and lays her back gently on the ground. Loud music. Camera starts to move rapidly with him as he runs out of the farmyard. CORINNE, who has been hiding inside a barn, runs out after him and they pelt away across the green fields, KALFON returning the attackers' fire with his pistol. He takes CORINNE by the arm as they run off into the distance. Fade out.

TITLE red letters : VENDÉ
MIAIRE*

The music continues over.

Close-up of KALFON's closed fist. He is wearing his military tunic with embroidered cuffs. (Still on page 79.)

KALFON off : *When your foot slips on a frog, you feel disgusted. But when you barely touch the human body* . . . He opens his hand to reveal a small frog crouched in his palm . . . *the skin of your fingers splits like scales of mica under hammer blows* . . .

CORINNE off : *Really?*

KALFON closing his fist on the frog : *Yes* . . .

We are back at the revolutionaries' camp. KALFON is sitting on the left with CORINNE just behind him. He is bearded, with dark glasses, wearing his military tunic and scarlet boots. He has his wrist in a sling. In the background, the blood-stained ERNEST is busying himself in the field kitchen.

KALFON : . . . *And just as a shark's heart beats for an hour after its death, so our insides still stir through and through, long after making love.*

CORINNE : *Why? I don't see* . . .

KALFON : *Because of the boundless horror which man feels for others*

---

* The first month in the Republican calendar (22nd September to 21st October).

of his species. Perhaps I may be wrong when I say this. But perhaps I may be right too . . . I know that there must probably exist a more terrible affliction than the swollen eyes which come from meditating on the strangeness of man's nature, but I have yet to discover it. He calls to the chef : *Well, Ernest?*

ERNEST, who has been poking at something in a large frying pan cooking over the fire, now hurries across with it and offers it to the couple. (Still on page 80.) They both help themselves to large chunks of meat and start to gnaw at them.

Close-up of CORINNE gnawing at a large bone. She is now wearing a flowered headband and looks exactly like the other hippies. (Still on page 80.)

CORINNE flicking the grease off her hands : *Not bad* . . . She takes another bite.

KALFON off : *Yes, we mixed the pig with the remains of the English tourists.*

CORINNE turning to him : *The ones in the Rolls?*

KALFON off : *That's right. There should be the left-overs of your husband in it too.*

CORINNE does not turn a hair, but just goes on gnawing at her bone. Then she turns to the chef off-screen and says :

CORINNE : *When I've finished, Ernest, I wouldn't mind a bit more.*

TITLE blue letters :
END OF STORY   /   END OF CINEMA*

---

* End of reel eleven.

WIND FROM THE EAST

by

Jean-Luc Godard and Jean-Pierre Gorin

WIND FROM THE EAST
OR GODARD AND ROCHA AT THE CROSSROADS

by James Roy Macbean

Near the middle of Godard's *Vent d'Est* (*Wind from the East*), there is a sequence where Brazilian film-maker Glauber Rocha plays a brief but symbolically important role. As Rocha stands with arms outstretched at a dusty crossroads, a young woman with a movie-camera comes up one of the paths (and the fact that she is very evidently pregnant is undoubtedly 'pregnant' with meaning). She goes up to Rocha and says very politely : 'Excuse me for interrupting your class struggle, but could you please tell me the way towards political cinema?'

Rocha points first in front of him, then behind him and to his left, and he says : 'That way is the cinema of aesthetic adventure and philosophical enquiry, while this way is the Third World cinema — a dangerous cinema, divine and marvellous, where the questions are practical ones like production, distribution, training 300 film-makers to make 600 films a year for Brazil alone, to supply one of the world's biggest markets.'

The woman starts off down the path to the Third World, when the inexplicable appearance of a red plastic ball seems to discourage her from proceeding in this direction. She takes a half-hearted kick at the ball, which rolls back to her anyway, as if it were doggedly insisting on following her — like Lamorisse's famous 'red balloon', which it resembles — and she then doubles back behind Glauber Rocha, who is still standing at the crossroads with arms outspread like a scarecrow or a crucified Christ without a cross. She sets out anew along the path of aesthetic adventure and philosophical enquiry.

I choose to begin an analysis of *Vent d'Est* by describing this brief sequence and suggesting some of its tongue-in-cheek symbolism because I believe it to be of critical importance, not just for an understanding of what Godard is trying to do in this film but also for an understanding of the way certain very important issues are shaping up in the vanguard of contemporary cinema. The presence of Rocha in this sequence is particularly significant; but the issues involved certainly go beyond just Godard and Rocha — and ultimately it may well be cinema itself which now stands at a critical crossroads.

For Rocha, the present intellectual crisis in Western Europe over the usefulness of art is senseless and politically negative. He sees the European artist — best exemplified by Godard — as having worked himself into a dead end, and he concludes that where cinema is concerned, the Third World may be the only place where an artist can still fruitfully go about the task of making films. Godard, on the other hand, reproaches Rocha for having 'a producer's mentality', for thinking too much in so-called 'practical' terms of distribution, markets, etc., thereby perpetuating the capitalist structures of cinema by extending them to the Third World—and in the process, neglecting urgent theoretical questions that must be asked if Third World cinema is to avoid merely repeating the ideological errors of Western cinema.

Godard deplores the way in which cinema, right from its birth, has been disfigured by a bourgeois capitalist ideology that permeates its very theoretical foundations and has never been correctly diagnosed, much less corrected. In *Vent d'Est,* therefore, he systematically takes apart the traditional elements of bourgeois cinema — especially as exemplified by the Western — revealing the sometimes hidden, sometimes blatant repressiveness which underlies it. What Godard attacks in *Vent d'Est* is what he calls 'the bourgeois concept of representation', which encompasses not only a certain acting style but also the traditional relations between image and sound — and ultimately, of course, the relations between the film and the audience.

Godard accuses bourgeois cinema of over-emphasising and playing on the deep-seated emotional fears and desires of the audience at the expense of their critical intelligence. He seeks to combat this tyranny of the emotions, not because he is 'against' emotions and 'for' rationality, nor because he is opposed to people's attitudes and actions being influenced by their experience of art; quite the contrary. But he believes strongly that the filmgoer should not be taken advantage of, that he should not be *manipulated* emotionally but should instead be addressed directly in a lucid dialogue which calls forth all of his human faculties.

The way things now stand, however, every element of a bourgeois film is carefully calculated to invite the viewer to indulge in the 'lived' emotional experience of a so-called 'slice of life' instead of assuming a critical, analytical and, ultimately, *political* attitude towards what he sees and hears. Why should one's attitude towards a film be political, one might ask? The answer is, of course, that the invitation to indulge in emotion at the expense of rational analysis already constitutes a political act — and implies a political attitude on the part of the viewer, without the viewer necessarily being even aware of it.

For one thing, by letting himself be emotionally 'moved' by the cinema — and even demanding that cinema should be emotionally moving — the filmgoer puts himself at the mercy of anyone who comes along with a lot of money to invest in seeing to it that filmgoers are 'moved'. And the people who have that kind of money also have a vested interest in making sure that audiences are 'moved' in the right direction — that is, in the direction of perpetuating the investor's advantageous position in an economic system which permits gross inequities in the distribution of wealth. In short, cinema (as well as television) functions as an ideological weapon used by the ruling-owning class to extend the market for the dreams which it sells.

Moreover, as Godard asserts in *Vent d'Est,* cinema tries to pass off bourgeois dreams as reality, and even plays on the heightening and enhancing effect of cinema in an effort to make us believe that these dreams depicted on our movie screens are somehow 'larger than life', that they are not only 'real' but somehow 'more real than the real'. In bourgeois cinema, all conspires to this effect: the acting style is at the same time 'realistic' and 'larger than life'; the decors are 'realistic' (or, if filmed on locations, simply real), but they are also carefully selected for their beauty and their 'larger than life' aspect. Likewise for the costumes, clothing, jewellery and make-up worn by the actors and actresses, who, themselves, are carefully selected for their 'larger than life' aspect. Finally, even sound is used to give us the illusion that we are eavesdropping on a moment of 'reality' where the characters are oblivious of our presence and are simply living out their 'real-life' emotions.

Since *Weekend,* Godard has rejected conventional film dialogue because he finds that it contributes to this misguided illusion of 'reality' and makes it all the easier for the viewer-listener to imagine himself right up there with the people on the screen, present yet 'safe', in a perfect position (that of an eavesdropper and peeping Tom) to participate vicariously in the emotion of the moment. In short, the bourgeois cinema pretends to ignore the presence of the spectator, pretends that what is being said and done on the movie screen is not aimed at the spectator, pretends that the cinema is a 'reflection of reality'; yet all the time it plays on his emotions and capitalises on his identification-projection mechanisms in order to induce him, subtly, insidiously, unconsciously, to participate in the dreams and fantasies that are marketed by bourgeois capitalist society.

There is an excellent sequence in *Vent d'Est* where Godard demonstrates and demystifies what takes place behind the façade of bourgeois cinema. On the sound-track we are told that 'In ten seconds you will see and hear a typical character in bourgeois cinema. He is in every film and he always plays a Don Juan type. He will describe the room you are sitting in.' We then see a close-up of a very handsome young Italian actor, standing at the edge of a swift-running stream and looking directly into the camera. Behind him — but photographed so that depth-perception is greatly reduced and the image as a whole is markedly flat — rises the grassy green slope of the opposite bank.

The young man speaks in Italian, while voices on the sound-track give us a running translation in both French and English. The translation, however, is rendered 'indirectly': the voice tells us, 'He says the room is dark. He sees people sitting downstairs and also up in the balcony. He says there is an ugly old fogey over there, all wrinkled; and over here he says he has spotted a good-looking young chick. He says he would like to lay her. He asks her to come up on the screen with him. He says it's beautiful up there, with the sun shining and the green trees all around and lots of happy people having a good time. He says if you don't believe him, look . . .' And at that point the camera suddenly moves back and slightly upward, keeping the young man in focus in the righthand corner of the frame while it reveals on the left side — and what seems like almost a hundred feet below the young man — a breathtakingly beautiful scene of a waterfall spilling into a natural pool in a shaded glen where young people are diving and swimming in the clear water.

It's a magnificent shot. The image itself is extremely beautiful, and most amazing of all is the very complex restructuring of space accomplished by such a simple camera movement. But if we think about this sequence and its dazzling denouement, we realise that everything in it is a calculated come-on aimed at the dreams and fantasies of the audience. The man is young and handsome. When he speaks, he disparages age and ugliness and glorifies youth and glamour. What he wants is sex, what he offers is sex. On the screen, he assures us, everything is beautiful and people are happy.

And that sudden restructuring of space literally invites us into the image all by itself. Like bourgeois cinema in general, it presents the bourgeois capitalist world as one of great depth, inexhaustibly rich and endlessly inviting. And the bourgeois cinema's predilection for depth-of-field photography (see Bazin) emphasises the 'you are there' illusion and thereby masks its own presence (and its act of presenting this image) behind a self-effacing false modesty calculated to make cinema appear to be the humble servant of 'reality' itself instead of what it really is — the not at all humble lackey of the capitalist ruling class. The audience is flirted with, coaxed and cajoled into coming up on the screen to join the 'beautiful people' for a little sex and leisure amid beautiful surroundings. And the thing which really clinches the deal is the stunning virtuosity of the camera in providing visual thrills.

Once again, this raises the problem of visual beauty in 'political' cinema; but it also demonstrates how Godard uses visual beauty in new ways that serve to demystify (and make us less vulnerable to) the old uses of visual beauty in bourgeois cinema. Later, a similar alerting of our critical faculties occurs in the sequence where the cavalry officer rides around on horseback clubbing the recalcitrant prisoners — another scene which Rocha finds extremely beautiful but which he criticises for not turning out to be brutal the way he (and even Ventura, who was the sound man for *Vent d'Est*) thinks the scene was intended. What Godard does in this sequence is to utilise a few of the techniques so often employed by the bourgeois cinema for this type of violent action sequence — turning the sound volume way up and continually making abrupt camera movements. The effect of these devices is usually a high emotional intensity and a very visceral sense of violence and confusion. (Remember their use in *Tom Jones*.) But Godard has made one major variation on these elements which completely changes our relation to this sequence.

His camera does continually make abrupt movements, but it also traces a very precise formal pattern — swinging abruptly about 35° left then 35° right, back and forth several times, then abruptly swinging about 35° up, then 35° down, and so on, exploring in a very formal way the closed space of the lush ravine where the action takes place. The purely formal quality of these camera movements (Rocha admiringly proclaimed them 'unprecedented in the whole history of film ') effectively distances us from the action and prevents us from reacting to it emotionally. In short, this sequence is not meant to be brutal, but it is meant to call our attention to the way bourgeois cinema would make it brutal — and in so doing, brutalise us.

But the way things stand now, the filmgoer rarely seems to look upon the cinema as a dialogue between himself and the film, and he relinquishes all too readily his own active part in that dialogue and hands over the tool of dialogue exclusively to the people in the film. And the more emotionally charged is the dialogue in the film, the more the viewer is ' moved ' by it. In *Vent d'Est,* however, this habitual passivity is challenged from the outset, as Godard gives us an opening shot that arouses our curiosity (a young man and woman are seen lying motionless on the ground, their arms bound together by a heavy chain) but systematically thwarts our expectations by simply holding the shot for nearly eight minutes without any action (the young man does stir enough gently to touch the face of the young woman at one point) and without dialogue. In fact, when the voice-over ' commentary ' finally breaks in (on the ' forest murmurs ' we have been hearing), what we get is not dialogue but the critique of dialogue.

Ostensibly talking about strike tactics in some labour dispute, the speaker states at one point that what is needed is dialogue, but that dialogue is usually handed over to a ' qualified representative ' who translates the demands of the workers into the language of the bosses, and in so doing betrays the people he supposedly represents. This voice-over discussion of the failure of dialogue clearly refers to the bargaining dialogues that go on between labour and capital; and a few minutes later, in the next sequence, there is a demonstration (in the style of a Western movie) of the way the ' qualified representative ' (the union delegate) distorts the real demands of the workers (for revolutionary overthrow of the capitalist system which exploits them) by translating those demands into terms the bosses can deal with (higher wages, shorter hours, better working conditions, etc.). But in a strange and insightful way, this discussion of the failure of dialogue in the hands of a ' qualified representative ' also refers to the failure of dialogue within the ' bourgeois concept of representation ' in the cinema.

' What is needed is dialogue ': this statement in the voice-over ' commentary ' seems to echo our own thoughts as we watch this exasperatingly long, static and dialogue-less shot. We are impatient to 'get into the movie ', we are impatient to get on with the plot. We wonder why the young couple are lying on the ground and why they are chained together. We wish they would at least regain consciousness enough to start talking to one another so that we could find out, from their dialogue, what is happening — that is, what is happening *to them*. As usual, in the cinema, we don't ask ourselves what is happening *to us*. We don't ask ourselves why a film addresses *us* in this particular way or that. In fact, we rarely think of a film as addressing us or, for that matter, anyone at all. We sit back and accept the tacit understanding that a film is a ' reflection of reality ' captured in the mirror of that magical ' eye of God ' that is a movie-camera. We sit back passively and wait for a film to lead us by the hand — or, more literally, by the heart.

We relinquish our dialogue with the film; and when this happens the film no longer speaks with us, or even to us, but instead speaks *for us,* in our place. And in bourgeois capitalist society, film (like television) speaks the language of big business, which seeks constantly to shove more goods down our gullets, to get us to like being force-fed, to get us to desire the very state of affairs which perpetuates our exploited and alienated condition. In letting a film speak for us, we allow our real needs to be distorted into the ersatz needs big business wants us to have. We are accomplices in our own betrayal.

What is to be done, then, to get us out of this deplorable situation? As the voice-over speaker in *Vent d'Est* puts it : ' Today the question "what is to be done " is urgently asked of militant film-makers. It is no longer a question of what path to take; it is a question of what one should do practically on a path that the history of revolutionary struggles has helped us to recognise. To make a film, for example, is to ask oneself the question "where do we stand ". And what does this question mean for a militant film-maker? It means, first but not exclusively, opening a parenthesis in which we ask ourselves what the history of revolutionary cinema can teach us.'

There then follows a most interesting rundown on some of the high points and weak spots of what could be qualified as revolutionary cinema — beginning with the young Eisenstein's admiration for D. W. Griffiths' *Intolerance*. Throughout this brief ' bird's-eye view ' of revolutionary cinema there runs the unifying thread of the necessity of thinking through very thoroughly the theoretical foundations of one's cinematic *praxis*. If we (along with Godard) can learn anything from the history of revolutionary cinema, it is clearly that constant self-critical vigilance is necessary if a film-maker is to avoid playing unwittingly into the hands of the opposition. And if a film-maker's commitment to revolutionary liberation is more than just an emotional identification with the oppressed, then his cinematic practice must address itself to more than just the emotions and identification-projection mechanisms of the audience. If he is firmly convinced (as Godard is) that the process of revolutionary liberation involves far more than just the revenge of the persecuted, and that it offers the concrete possibility of putting an end to persecution (in other words, of creating an objectively more *just* society in which the free development of his fellow man), then it is the film-maker's urgent task to create cinematic forms which, themselves, work for rather than against the free development of the spectator, forms which do not manipulate his emotions or his unconscious but which provide him with an analytical tool to utilise in dealing with the complexity of the present.

Godard's recent films are politically pointed, to be sure; but although the verbal 'commentary' is prominent——if not pre-eminent—the films are not exhortatory. There is nothing demagogic in Godard's approach either to cinema or to politics. A film like *Vent d'Est* is at the opposite pole in cinematic method from either Riefenstahl's *Triumph of the Will* or Eisenstein's *Potemkin*. And for that matter, Godard's *British Sounds, Pravda* and *Vent d'Est* are far removed in cinematic method from Rocha's *Black God, White Devil, Land in a Trance* and *Antonio das Mortes*. There is a strong messianic tone in Rocha's films that is very alien to Godard's way of constructing a film. (It is quite clear, by the way, that Rocha's outstretched arms in *Vent d'Est*—suggesting a parallel between Rocha and Christ — constitute Godard's ironic comment on the messianic aspects of Rocha's film style.)

And while both Rocha and Godard are committed to the worldwide struggle for revolutionary liberation, they clearly have very divergent opinions about how revolution can develop and how cinema can contribute to that development. Rocha takes the 'spontaneous' approach and largely discounts the importance of theoretical concerns, which he considers mere 'auxiliaries' to the spontaneous energy of the masses. He has expressed his belief that: 'The true revolutionaries in South America are individuals, suffering personalities, who are not involved in theoretical problems . . . the provocation to violence, the contact with bitter reality that may eventually produce violent change in

South America, this upheaval can only come from individual people who have suffered themselves and who have realised that a need for change is present—not for theoretical reasons but because of personal agony.'* And Rocha emphasises his belief that the real strength of the South American masses lies in *mysticism,* in 'an emotional, Dionysiac behaviour' which he sees as arising from a mixture of Catholicism and African religions. The energy which has its source in mysticism, Rocha argues, is what will ultimately lead the people to resist oppression — and it is this emotional energy which he seeks to tap in his films.

Godard, on the other hand, rejects the emotional approach as one which plays into the hand of the enemy and seeks to combat mystification in any form, whether from the Right or the Left. While there is no indication that Godard underestimates the importance of the agonised personal experience of oppression as a starting-point for the development of revolutionary consciousness, he clearly takes the position that solidly developed organisation on sound theoretical foundations is needed if the revolutionary movement is to advance beyond the stage of abortive, short-lived, 'spontaneous' uprisings (like the May 1968 events in France).

And in emphasising the theoretical struggle, Godard follows in the path of no less a practical revolutionary than Lenin himself, who in his pamphlet entitled *What Is to be Done?* (echoes of which abound in *Vent d'Est*), roundly castigated the 'cult of spontaneity' and pointed out that *'any* cult of spontaneity, any weakening of the "element of lucid awareness" . . . *signifies* in itself—*and whether one wants it this way or not is immaterial—a reinforcing of the influence of bourgeois ideology.'† [Italics are Lenin's.] Or, as Lenin puts it a few lines further on : 'The problem poses itself in these terms and no others : bourgeois ideology or socialist ideology. There is no middle ground (for humanity has never set up a 'third' ideology; and, in any case, where society is torn by class-struggle, there could never be an ideology above and beyond class).' And later, 'But why—asks the reader—does the spontaneous movement, which tends towards the direction of the least effort, lead precisely to domination by bourgeois ideology? For the simple reason that, chronologically, bourgeois ideology is much older than socialist ideology, that it is much more thoroughly elaborated, and that it possesses infinitely more means of diffusion.' And finally, 'The greater the spontaneous spirit of the masses, and the more the movement is widespread, then all the more urgent is the necessity of the utmost lucidity in our theoretical work, our political work and our organising.'‡

Lest anyone be tempted, by the way, to jump to the conclusion (one which Rocha seems to encourage in his article on *Vent d'Est*) that the differences of opinion on revolutionary strategy between Godard and Rocha are simply the result of cultural differences between the European world-view and that of the Third World, it should be pointed out that even in the South American cinema there is nowhere near unanimous support for the 'spontaneous' approach. South American film-makers are increasingly following the lead of the Argentine film-maker Fernando Solanas (*La Hora de los Hornos*) in calling for an intensification of the theoretical struggle at the level of ideology.

It must be understood, however, that Rocha has a legitimate gripe when he complains of the flood of imitation-Godard monstrosities being turned out by self-indulgent film students in the Third World and everywhere. But the blame is hardly Godard's. (Does anyone doubt for a moment that these same students would be turning out self-indulgent monstrosities whether Godard existed or not?) Moreover, if there is anything which could effectively combat the sort of mindless self-indulgence which characterises not only most student films but quite simply most films in general, surely it is the very thorough, resolute and self-disciplined *theoretical praxis* embodied by the films of Jean-Luc Godard.

I use the expression *theoretical praxis* quite pointedly, for I want to emphasise that *theory* and *practice* are by no means mutually exclusive. To illustrate what I mean, let us pick up once more, by way of a conclusion the 'crossroads' metaphor. Godard's path — which, as he points out, is simply the path which study of the history or revolutionary cinema has helped him to recognise—is the path of creating the theoretical foundations of revolutionary cinema within the day-to-day practice of making films. The real dilemma for film-makers today is not a choice between theory and practice. The act of making films necessarily combines both—and this is true whether one makes films in the Third World, Russia or the West.

In *Vent d'Est's* 'crossroads' sequence, there is even a strong visual suggestion that the three-way intersection is simply the point where two paths—that of the Third World and that which the European woman with a movie-camera has travelled up to this point—converge and join together in what is really one big ongoing path of 'aesthetic adventure and philosophical enquiry'; which, by necessity, combines both theory and practice.

* Quoted from 'The Way to Make a Future: A Conversation with Glauber Rocha', by Gordon Hitchens. *Film Quarterly,* Fall 1970.

† Lenin, *Que Faire?* Editions Sociales, Paris, 1969. All translations from the French edition are by the present author.

‡ This latter statement comes closest to Lenin's later qualification of the position adopted in *What Is to be Done?*—which position, as he indicated, was a tactical response arising from a concrete analysis of a concrete situation (the 1902 squabbles among diverse factions of the left). Later, when the potential dangers of the spontaneous position were no longer as much of a threat to the revolution, Lenin toned down the attack on spontaneity and called for a more dialectical approach of 'organised spontaneity and spontaneous organisation.' (For excellent material on this, see the special Lenin-Hegel issue of *Radical America,* September-October, 1970.)

CREDITS :

Original title	Vent d'Est/Vento Dell' Est
Script by	Jean-Luc Godard and Jean-Pierre Gorin
Directed by	Jean-Luc Godard and Jean-Pierre Gorin
Produced by	Gianni Barcelloni, Ettore Rosboch
Production company	Poli Film (Rome)/Anouchka Films (Paris)/CCC (Berlin)
Director of photography	Mario Vulpiano
Colour process	Eastman Colour
Length	3,420 feet (16 mm.)
Running time	95 minutes
Made on locations in	Italy, May 1969
Shown at	Cannes Festival, Directors' Fortnight, 1970, and New York Festival, 1970

CAST :

Gian Maria Volonte
Anna Wiazemsky
Glauber Rocha
Jean-Luc Godard
George Götz
Christian Tullio

WIND FROM THE EAST

A couple are seen from above lying motionless in a field, their wrists bound together by a chain. The girl — ANNA WIAZEMSKY — wears a flounced white petticoat which fans out on the ground about her. (Still on page 145.) After some time another girl's voice is heard over.

FEMALE VOICE over : *We went to see my father's family in May as we did every year. My uncle managed the exploitation of aluminium for the Alcoa company near Dodge City. We stayed some way out of town on an estate he had bought from the bank manager. The house itself lay in the middle of a park surrounded by a white fence. It wasn't a big house, but it was so full of unexpected corners that we never grew tired of exploring it. Every night we dined from eight to twelve. On Friday my uncle did not return home. We waited the whole night for him. It was Saturday lunchtime before we heard that the miners had locked him in his office.*

MALE VOICE over : *Strike. Strike.*

UNION DELEGATE over : *Listen, you're jumping to conclusions. Just think it over; things don't happen by themselves. There was already general discontent about the bad working conditions.*

MALE VOICE over : *The union delegate.*

WIAZEMSKY moves her head on the ground.

FEMALE VOICE over : *My father would not let us go out any more; the workers were very restive and anything could have happened. One evening in the library I overheard a conversation between my father and Uncle Sam. My father said that times had changed, that the workers earned much more and worked less and that since the formation of trade unions, the employer was exploited more than the employee. The workers even ate chicken every Saturday. They should be made to work hard and live in uncomfortable homes, because they didn't suffer from it as much as we would. Anyway, my father went on, shrugging his shoulders, nobody died of hunger. And if the workers hate the bourgeoisie, it must mean they are jealous, and jealousy is a*

121

mean feeling. Uncle Sam agreed with my father in theory but not in practice: he reckoned that you had to negotiate, but with the right people.

MALE VOICE over : *The union delegate.*

UNION DELEGATE over : *The real workers were against any kind of unrest. And we support this position.*

MALE VOICE over : *Revisionism.*

UNION DELEGATE over : *We do not support violence. We will not break the rules of democracy. We believe that it is possible to change society peacefully.*

FIRST FEMALE VOICE over : *Yes, but, listen now, in spite of everything . . .*

SECOND FEMALE VOICE over : *Social democracy.*

FIRST FEMALE VOICE over : *. . . incredible things seem to be happening, though I know you have no part in them. Who poisoned the horses? Who set fire to the printing works? Who looted the Nixon Hotel, because the proprietor threatened them? Then there's this school-teacher lady who says you've got to be open to new ideas. Well, she lives according to them. Do you want to know what I think? She's a whore!*

UNION DELEGATE over : *But if things had not been so serious, everything these pseudo-revolutionaries said and did would have seemed ludicrous. But you are right really, we shouldn't underestimate the effect of their shameful activities, which create unrest, doubt and scepticism among a lot of the workers, especially the younger ones. In fact, their activities are part of a series of lies uttered without the consent of the true representatives of the people's interests.*

WIAZEMSKY rubs her face on her arm.

FIRST FEMALE VOICE over : *Yes, but listen . . .*

The scene changes to a dusty white road sloping past a primitive building with a tiled roof; the walls are splashed and streaked with a rusty red.

FIRST FEMALE VOICE over : *There are still a lot of very strange things happening, which were unthinkable three months ago.*

MALE VOICE over : *The active minorities.*

FIRST FEMALE VOICE over : *The people are frightened by this wave of violence. It's difficult to tell whether the revolution is going to spread or not. Like all reasonable people, I'm very puzzled by all this. Only this morning my servant said to me: ' It's got to stop; we've had enough violence.'*

As she finishes speaking a bearded man carrying a rifle — the CAVALRYMAN — strolls across the shot from the left. He looks around, picks up his greatcoat from a treetrunk and walks off to the right. Country noises, the twittering of birds etc., are heard loudly.

SECOND FEMALE VOICE over : *In what we have just heard, there are two voices which lie and two which stammer . . .*

We return to the couple from another angle, half hidden by branches in the foreground. They are embracing tenderly and the YOUNG MAN is stroking WIAZEMSKY'S hair.

SECOND FEMALE VOICE over : *The stammering voices talk about striking, social democracy, revisionism, active minorities and general assemblies. The lying voices talk about the desperate state of affairs, general dissatisfaction, good people who are frightened and honest workers.*

UNION DELEGATE over : *Quite right. But where will all this stupid violence get us? They've destroyed the printing works. Result: no more objective news. They've set fire to the Nixon Hotel. Result: the businessmen are frightened and have formed armed groups, supported with money from the banks. In fact, it's all the leftists' fault that the monopolists have gained control of everything. We've got to get rid of these* provocateurs; *they're the reactionaries' best agents.*

MALE VOICE over : *Repression.*

UNION DELEGATE over : *We condemn the brutal repression of the workers. We demand its immediate cessation. We want the prisoners freed and total disarmament. We demand that all armed bands be disarmed and that the talks about the future . . . the future of the city should be reopened. After Saturday night's shooting, we have decided to open the fight against authority by calling . . . by calling a two-hour general strike and organizing demonstrations which people will not fail to take an active part in. Stop the repression. Freedom; freedom; democracy. But just what is going on? What is going on? Tell me! You block work like this, in front of the factory, without telling your comrades? You are behaving like children! If you go on like this, you'll end up worse off, if not dead! Is that what you want? Civil war? So stop fooling about. Trust those who are responsible for you. That's what we're here for.*

MALE VOICE over : *Active strike.*

Another view of the red-washed building silhouetted against the sky. Beside it is a ruined wall with trees growing behind it. As the voices continue over, the CAVALRYMAN wanders to and fro on the wall in an aimless ritual, keeping watch for a non-existent enemy.

FIRST FEMALE VOICE over: *I told you things were going from bad to worse. You'll be completely overpowered, too. If it comes to that, there's only the army left.*

SECOND FEMALE VOICE over: *The two voices have continued to lie; the two others have continued to stammer. Which one is speaking for us? How can we find out? Today, the militant film-maker asks this question: 'What must we do?' As far as he is concerned, it is not a question of choosing a course of action, but of actually creating a course. He has to decide how to do this according to the history of re-volutionary conflict.* Long pause. *Yes, what must we do? Make a film for instance. That means asking yourself: 'Where are we now?' And what does it mean for the militant film-maker to ask himself the ques-tion: 'Where are we now?'* Long pause. *And what does it mean for the militant film-maker to ask himself the question: 'Where are we now?' It means first of all setting yourself free of other influences and devoting yourself to the history of the revolutionary cinema . . . of the revolutionary cinema.*

A medium close-up shows a GIRL wearing a red sweater, her hair clipped back, having her face made up for filming. Countryside noises continue as camera tracks right to show a man in a white open-necked shirt, streaking his face with brightly coloured make-up from a tube. He will be the INDIAN.

SECOND FEMALE VOICE over: *Victory of the revolutionary cinema (July 19, 1920). After the speech made by Comrade Lenin at the Second Congress of the Third Internationale, Comrade Dziga Vertov declared from the platform: 'We bolshevist film makers know that it is impossible for a film to exist outside the context of the class system. We know that the actual production of films is only of secondary importance . . .'*

Camera tracks slowly back to the GIRL again as the make-up assistant bends down in front of her.

SECOND FEMALE VOICE over: *' . . . Our programme is very simple: to see and show the world in the name of the people's world revolu-tion . . .'*

Close-up of the GIRL's face as the make-up assistant dusts it off

124

with a camel hair brush. Her hair is now hanging loose, as she stares straight at the camera.

SECOND FEMALE VOICE over: *'The people make history. The films of the Western hemisphere only portray elegant ladies and gentlemen.* The GIRL smiles — a careful, rehearsed smile. *Actors are forced to express the corrupt ideas of the bourgeoisie; under the cover of make-up, they unscrupulously depict the degenerate ways of bourgeois life. All this is done with the excuse that they are expressing fundamental feelings and instincts!'*

Resume on medium close-up; the GIRL now has her hair clipped back again. She looks critically in her hand mirror and then opens her mouth as the make-up assistant starts to apply make-up to her lips. Then camera tracks slowly sideways to the INDIAN on the right, his face grotesquely streaked with red, white, blue and yellow. (Still on page 145.)

SECOND FEMALE VOICE over: *Defeat for the revolutionary cinema (November 18, 1924). A few days after the death of Lenin, Sergei Eisenstein was deeply moved by a performance of* Intolerance, *a film by the American imperialist Griffith. Result: mistaking primary duty for secondary duty, Eisenstein produced a film about the sailors of the battleship* Potemkin, *instead of glorifying the people's struggle of the moment. Result: in 1929, in* The General Line, *while Eisenstein uses new terms to describe agrarian reforms during the Tsarist oppression, he still uses old expressions to talk about collectivism. In his case, this is the final victory of the old over the new. Result: Hollywood paid for his journey to film the Mexican revolution, while in Berlin, Dr. Goebbels, one of the leaders of the Nazi party, ordered a Nazi* Potemkin.

We now see the UNION DELEGATE — a bearded man in turn-of-the-century costume, wearing tinted spectacles and a richly patterned jacket. He stands amid greenery, reading aloud, from a paperback by Waldeck-Rochet. Instead of his voice, the voice over continues.

SECOND FEMALE VOICE over: *The dialectic of history is such that the triumph of Marxism on the theoretical level forces its enemies to pose as Marxists, to pose as Marxists, to pose as Marxists, to pose as Marxists, to pose as Marxists, to pose as Marxists.*

Resume on the INDIAN as he mixes different coloured greasepaints before applying them to the underside of his chin. Then camera tracks slowly across to the GIRL, now having her eyes made up;

she raises the hand mirror and she and the make-up assistant check her appearance in it before continuing.

SECOND FEMALE VOICE over: *Defeat of the revolutionary film (November 17, 1935). Speech by Comrade Stalin at the First Conference of Russian Stakhanoviks: confused by the obscurity of this speech, Comrade Dziga Vertov forgets that politics command the economy. His film* The Eleventh Year *became a hymn to economic progress, instead of being an ode to the eleven-year-old dictatorship of the proletariat. It was then that revisionism finally found its way into the Soviet cinema.*

Camera tracks across to the INDIAN again. He places a dab of red in the centre of his forehead, then picks up a tube of white grease-paint. Woodland noises — the chirping of birds, rushing water — continue off.

Close-up: he stands with one arm raised across his forehead, his face a grotesque mask of thickly applied greasepaint — red, yellow, green and blue.

SECOND FEMALE VOICE over: *The revolution advances in disguise.*

Resume on the GIRL being made up; an assistant holds up a clapper-board reading 42 — VENTO DELL' EST in front of her, then goes off.

SECOND FEMALE VOICE over: *False victory of the revolutionary cinema (August 29, 1962): the progressive states of Africa renounced all initiative and elected to rely on the Western film industry for their films, thus giving white Christians the right to talk about Negroes and Arabs. Algiers — Pontecorvo, Klein; Konakry — Société Comaçico.*

Camera shifts slightly from side to side; white screen, then we return to the same scene; the man holds up the clapperboard again, now reading 42 — 1, then disappears, while the make-up assistant continues working on the GIRL's face.

SECOND FEMALE VOICE over: *While civil wars and popular movements bring the imperialists down, they creep back via the camera, thus endangering the revolution.*

A low angle shot shows the CAVALRYMAN and the GIRL from the previous scenes, who is now in period costume. They are by the wall of the shack seen earlier, eating from a plate which the CAVALRYMAN holds out between them. He looks upwards as he masticates reflectively.

SECOND FEMALE VOICE over: *The ideas of the ruling class always dominate the rest of the population. In other words, the financially privileged class which rules society is also the class with the most cultural influence . . .*

Another low angled shot shows the GIRL in her period dress, which is pink with elaborate frills and a bustle. Holding up a cine camera, she turns in a circle, then bends down to shoot something on the ground.

SECOND FEMALE VOICE over : *Cultural influence. The class which disposes of the material means of production also disposes of the intellectual means of production. Thus the ideas of those people who are deprived of the intellectual means of production can be said to be repressed by the ruling class.*

Resume on the GIRL as previously, still having her face made up; the make-up assistant leans over her, painting round her eyes.

SECOND FEMALE VOICE over : *Victory of the revolutionary cinema (February 2, 1956). Leading article in* Red Flag. *Comrade Tian-Tsin denounces the theory affirming that the truth must be written and denounces the theory of the great road of realism. She denounces the theory of the average man as protagonist. She denounces the theory of opposition to the decisive role of the subject.*

Camera tracks across to the INDIAN applying make-up to his face again.

SECOND FEMALE VOICE over : *Birth of the materialist feature film (February 2, 1956).*

Close-up of his face as before, beneath the mask of make-up.

SECOND FEMALE VOICE over : *We are never completely the contemporaries of our own times. History advances in disguise. It fills the screen with the mask of the preceding sequence, and we no longer recognize anything about the film. This is not the fault of history, but the fault of our range of vision, which is cluttered with images and sounds. We hear and see the past superimposed on the present, even though the present is the revolution.*

TITLE black and red letters :

WIND FROM
THE EAST

The scene changes to the edge of a wood. As the voice continues over, a procession of people in assorted costumes file into view between the bushes in the background.

SECOND FEMALE VOICE over: *The militant now asks himself very emphatically: 'What must I do?' It is not really a question of choosing a course of action, but rather of deciding what can be done practically in the field of action which has been indicated to them by the history of revolutionary theories and by history itself. And what have we achieved in this field of action — strikes, social democracy, general meetings, repression? Daring to recognize it, thinking about it, means knowing what to do.*

TITLE red and black letters and symbols:

1 — THE STRIKE

Resume on the shot of the edge of the wood. The people file out of the bushes towards us; at their head are ANNA WIAZEMSKY and the YOUNG MAN seen at the beginning of the film; behind them the UNION DELEGATE, now wearing a panama hat and accompanied by the GIRL in the pink dress; following them is the INDIAN dressed in a white costume with a red sash, and the CAVALRYMAN brings up the rear. Camera follows the procession as it moves towards the right; progress is hindered by the fact that every few steps the YOUNG MAN at the front stops dead and says 'Water!' WIAZEMSKY, in her white petticoat, fetches a bottle from the INDIAN and hands it to the YOUNG MAN, who drinks and hands it back again. This process is repeated several times.

MALE VOICE over: *Tuesday, June 3, 14.00 hours. On the initiative of several workers and after a good deal of discussion among the workers, it has been decided to call a general strike. The aims of the strike have been explained in a leaflet.*

YOUNG MAN stopping: *Water!*

WIAZEMSKY fetches the bottle.

MALE VOICE over: *The overtime allowance for most workers varies from 0 to 20 hours in two weeks. Some of us worked in pretty rough conditions to . . .*

YOUNG MAN stopping: *Water!*

WIAZEMSKY fetches the bottle again.

MALE VOICE over: *. . . get an allowance of between 0 and 10 hours, which comes to about 350 francs for two weeks. Right from the beginning, 80 per cent of the workers from the 13.00 — 22.00 hours shift supported the strike.*

YOUNG MAN stopping: *Water!*

As the sequence continues, the CAVALRYMAN comes up to the YOUNG MAN, grabs the bottle from him and hands it to WIAZEMSKY. He then hustles the YOUNG MAN off towards the left and shoves the INDIAN forward to take his place at the front of the procession.

MALE VOICE over: *On Wednesday morning at 4.30, the strikers demanded that the second-shift workers, who had not taken part in the discussions, should join the movement. At a later meeting of the workers from that shift, it was reported that a decision to strike had been made, supported by 90 per cent of the workers.*

Suddenly the INDIAN squats down on the ground and refuses to budge. The others circle round him, looking puzzled. The GIRL in the pink dress, who is carrying a parasol, hands him the water bottle and he drinks, but still does not move. WIAZEMSKY then fetches his moccasins which the CAVALRYMAN is carrying tucked into the pocket of his greatcoat. The INDIAN puts them on and gets up, then, after a moment's hesitation, sits down again.

MALE VOICE over: *On Thursday 5, at 5 in the morning, the strike committee decided to go on with the strike. Leaflets were distributed, appealing to the strikers: 'We carry on the strike until we win.'*

The CAVALRYMAN gets angry; he works the bolt on his rifle and pokes the INDIAN in the back with it, but the UNION DELEGATE hurries forward and restrains him. (Production still on page 146.)

MALE VOICE over: *'They are trying to divide the two shifts. Let's take our decisions together. Our grievances are the same.'*

Medium close-up of the INDIAN squatting on the ground. He looks up as the UNION DELEGATE pushes aside the CAVALRYMAN's rifle, bends down and shakes the INDIAN by the shoulder.

UNION DELEGATE in Italian: *What do you want?*

INDIAN in English: *Down with the ruling class! Power for the working class!*

The UNION DELEGATE pats him patronizingly on the shoulder and the camera tracks as he walks across to the CAVALRYMAN on the right.

CAVALRYMAN in Italian: *What does he want?*

UNION DELEGATE in Italian, fanning himself with his hat: *He wants better working conditions and more pay. You see, he is a poor Indian. His wife and sons are sick. In my opinion we can even come to an agreement . . . I can look into it . . . but . . . once we get to the*

129

camp . . .

CAVALRYMAN in Italian : *As you like. You are responsible for that. As long as he is taken to the concentration camp . . .*

Camera tracks back to the left as the CAVALRYMAN goes off, while the UNION DELEGATE stands over the INDIAN and pulls a coin out of his pocket. He puts the coin in the INDIAN's hand and pats it dismissively.

SECOND FEMALE VOICE over : *There are rumours of a strike . . .*

The UNION DELEGATE slaps the INDIAN on the shoulder then kicks him in the behind.

UNION DELEGATE in Italian : *Come on.*

Long shot of the scene. WIAZEMSKY and the YOUNG MAN are lying on the ground. The UNION DELEGATE goads the INDIAN to his feet and hustles him off to the right; the others get up and trail slowly after. Camera pans and tracks to follow them as they go off into the distance, down the grassy slope.

SECOND FEMALE VOICE over : *The rumours say that their claims will be met. Who started these rumours? The union delegate. They say that 80 per cent of the workers have gone back to work, that only a few are carrying on with the strike. Who started this rumour? The union delegate. They're talking about agitators. That's what the bosses say when the workers start the struggle. And who speaks for the bosses? The union delegate. The union delegate translates the struggle of the working class into the language of the employers. And when the union delegate does this translation, he is acting as a traitor. This situation cannot be explained away as pure chance, or as the fault of some individual or group, or as the result of circumstances or national traditions. There are definite reasons inherent in the economic planning and development of all capitalist countries which make this treachery possible. The failure of the union delegate is the failure of socialistic opportunism, the failure of social democracy: this is revisionism. This is a product of the so-called peaceful phase in the development of the workers' movement.*

Resume on medium close-up of the INDIAN squatting on the ground. The scene with the UNION DELEGATE is repeated, although we do not hear their voices.

SECOND FEMALE VOICE over : *During this period the workers' movement acquires certain weapons to carry on the struggle: recourse to the processes of parliament, use of economic and political mass orga-*

130

nizations within legally defined limits as well as the availability of a large workers' press. On the other hand, it is during this period that the tendency to deny the relevance of the class struggle and to approve the principle of social peace starts. Translation — treason.

The UNION DELEGATE stands talking to the CAVALRYMAN as previously.

Then, as the voice over continues we see the procession coming towards us in single file along a woodland path. The YOUNG MAN comes first, then the GIRL with her sunshade, followed by the INDIAN, WIAZEMSKY, the UNION DELEGATE and the CAVALRYMAN bringing up the rear. Camera pans to show them from behind as they cross a stream by a large boulder, the CAVALRYMAN holding his rifle above his head.

SECOND FEMALE VOICE over: *Certain groups within the working classes — the bureaucrats and aristocrats of the workers' movement who benefited from the fruits of the exploitation of the Third World and the advantageous position of their own country in the world markets — and their petit-bourgeois associates from the heart of the Communist Party, form the main social support for this tendency. And they have become the bearers of bourgeois influence on the proletariat.*

As they go off to the right the INDIAN appears behind the boulder, having dodged out of the file. He picks up a stone and hurls it towards the others off-screen.

Medium shot: the INDIAN slips into view from the left while the others stand round the CAVALRYMAN, who is lying back on the ground clutching his leg in agony. The UNION DELEGATE bends over him to help, but he shakes his head and reaches for his rifle.

TITLE black and red letters and symbols:

1 — THE STRIKE

2 — THE DELEGATE

Resume on the scene. The UNION DELEGATE shoves the prisoners off towards the right, then follows after them, while the CAVALRYMAN comes limping behind. Camera pans to show them from a low angle as they go off into the distance.

UNION DELEGATE over: *Not only have the military and repressive forces siding with the established power in no way disbanded, but the mass of people are opposed to continued revolutionary exploits. Many of their grievances have been satisfied. Today, to prepare work is a victory.*

SECOND FEMALE VOICE over : *Translation — treason. When the union delegate speaks, he lies. Example:*

The UNION DELEGATE is seen as previously, standing amid greenery, reading from Waldeck-Rochet.

UNION DELEGATE reading : ' *The task of the new political power, the working class and its associates, is the simultaneous creation of a new economy and a new way of life, that is, a socialist way of life. The realization of this grand and gigantic task requires the broadest and most active participation of the masses in the management of public affairs. Socialism does not only mean the liberation of the worker from capitalist exploitation: he represents and must create a democracy which is superior to all bourgeois democracy.*' He turns the page. ' *Encouraged by the results achieved so far and knowing the road which is still left to travel, we shall put all our energy into the fight . . .'*

MAN'S VOICE over : *That's wrong.*

UNION DELEGATE : ' *. . . and bring it to a victorious end . . .'*

MAN'S VOICE over : *That's wrong.*

UNION DELEGATE : ' *The work of the united vital forces in the nation . . .'*

We are now looking up a grassy slope towards the skyline. WIAZEMSKY and the YOUNG MAN, having evidently escaped from the others, come pelting down the slope towards us and throw themselves upon the ground.

SECOND FEMALE VOICE over : *He talks, he talks, he talks.*

FIRST FEMALE VOICE and MALE VOICE over : *Escapades, provocation, it's always the same. We were forced to do something because the person who claimed to represent us never did anything. What he did do was talk to the bosses.*

TITLE black and red letters and symbols : WHAT SHALL WE DO?

A high angle close-up shows the YOUNG MAN lying back in the grass, his hands shielding his eyes.

YOUNG MAN : *We need a different sort of strike.*

WIAZEMSKY off : *All you need do is write a pamphlet for the workers.*

YOUNG MAN : *We'll distribute it tomorrow at the factory gates.*

WIAZEMSKY off : *Then the students will see that the workers get up early.*

YOUNG MAN : *Then at least the students will see that the workers get up early.*

WIAZEMSKY off : *Then at least the workers will see that the students get up early.*

TITLE black letters on a scribbled red background : WHAT SHALL WE DO?

We see the couple sitting in the field. WIAZEMSKY is now wearing a red skirt and a white blouse. The YOUNG MAN gets up and walks round her as she talks. Instead of her voice, we hear the commentary.

SECOND FEMALE VOICE over : *What are we going to do? Think left. Read Lenin's text, which is generally used by the revisionists to show those of the Left up as agitators. Note that Lenin does not confound a secondary danger with a primary one. Agree with Lenin that the primary danger lies in social-democratic treason and the secondary one in leftism, the childish, infantile illness of Communism. Note that Lenin spoke for a left-wing workers' movement and not for a left-wing student movement. Starting from this, attack leftism whenever and wherever it occurs in Leninist positions . . . Leninist, Leninist, Leninist . . .*

TITLE black letters against a background of red horizontal lines : WHAT SHALL WE DO?

High angle close-up of WIAZEMSKY sitting in the field, shouting. WIAZEMSKY : *We must learn from past faults. This will be to everybody's advantage.*

YOUNG MAN off : *There are always people who struggle against the innovations of a revolution, believing that none of them will succeed.*

WIAZEMSKY : *You always stand in the way of a new revolutionary order . . .*

YOUNG MAN off : *. . . by looking for help and guidance in conventional standards and established customs.*

TITLE black letters against a scribbled red background : THE ACTIVE MINORITIES

Seen from behind, WIAZEMSKY pins a poster, on which the word UNION is written in red three times, to a treetrunk. Then she runs off to the right. The YOUNG MAN drops into view from the branches of the tree and runs off after her. Strains of *Addio Lugano Bella* are heard intermittently, sung to a guitar.

The music continues loudly as they run across a field towards us and scramble under a barbed wire fence. The YOUNG MAN pauses to pin a poster to the barbed wire, on which the word UNIONE is written twice.

Sounds of rushing water. We are back with the procession of prisoners, now minus the fugitive couple. We see their legs and feet as they cross a stone bridge over a rushing stream, in the middle of which is a red U daubed on the stone. The INDIAN and the GIRL in the pink dress pass by, then the CAVALRYMAN. The latter pauses, dips his foot in the water and tries to scrub out the letter.

We move to an idyllic country scene. Half hidden by trees and flowers the GIRL in the pink dress sits holding up her parasol while the UNION DELEGATE, in his richly patterned jacket, bends courteously over her.

SECOND FEMALE VOICE over: *This woman is called Suzanne Monet, wife of the famous painter Claude Monet. In 1903 she published an open letter in the* Figaro *to the President of the French Republic, protesting against the striking railwaymen who had forbidden her husband to enter the Gare Saint Lazare to finish his painting.*

As they converse the man fans himself with his hat and takes off his glasses, looking round at the scene.

SECOND FEMALE VOICE over: *1925: this woman is called Scarlett Faulkner from Louisville (Alabama). A known nymphomaniac, she accused Richard Laverell, Dick Clever and Eddie, a farmhand, of having raped her several times. The local chapter of the Klu-Klux-Klan immediately carried out the execution of the horrible criminals Laverell, Clever and Eddie. In 1936, this woman has become Ines Mussolini, married to the Spanish representative of the Schneider-Krupp group. She welcomed Franco's troops into Barcelona after they had taken Catalonia from the Anarchists and the workers' councils.*

The UNION DELEGATE picks a flower and offers it to the GIRL.

SECOND FEMALE VOICE over: *In 1969, she is called Rachel Darnev, graduated in chemical analysis from the Vise-Farben University in*

Nuremberg. She specializes in the napalming of Palestinian farmers in
the Naplouse and Gaza area, who refuse to leave their land.
Seen from above, the YOUNG MAN who escaped from the column
of prisoners daubs red paint onto a rock with his fingers in the
shape of a U. Suddenly he rolls over on his back as if dead, and
more red paint is splashed across him from off-screen.
We resume on the couple in the sunlit meadow. The UNION
DELEGATE fans himself with his hat again.
UNION DELEGATE over : *This man's name is René Andrieu. He was*
editor-in-chief of l'Humanité. *In 1871 he proposed to the Central*
Committee of the Paris Commune that the red flag and the tricolore
should be united. In response, a worker called Varland proposed that
he be shot. Disappointed, Andrieu escaped to Versailles . . . In 1933,
this man's name is Luigi Dubceck. As a member of the Politburo of
the KPD, the German Communist Party, he appealed to his comrades
to react peacefully and sensibly to the demonstration organized by
Nazi stormtroopers outside the offices of the newspaper Vorwelt . . .
In 1945, this man is called Maurice Duclos. He was one of three com-
munist ministers in de Gaulle's government. As such, he appealed to
all partisans to lay down their arms. A year later these weapons were
used by the employers to put down a strike organized by European
miners . . . In 1969, this man's name has become Vladimir Brezhnev.
As commander of the battleship Potemkin, *he offers his ship to*
Admiral Foster Dulles to help locate the remains of American spy-
planes shot down over North Korean territory.
A shot of the red-washed wall of the building seen previously,
with the word UNION painted on it with black letters. The
CAVALRYMAN passes in the foreground with his rifle slung over his
shoulder, followed by the GIRL with the parasol (Still on page 147)
and finally the INDIAN. The INDIAN stops and looks at the legend,
picks up a piece of clay from the ground and starts to add another
letter.

TITLE red letters over a scribbled black background : THE ACTIVE
MINORITIES

Resume on the wall of the building. The INDIAN adds an E to the
end of UNION and RI in front, then turns and runs off as a
shower of smoke and debris sprays at him as if there had been an
explosion off-screen.

135

TITLE red letters and symbols:

1 — THE STRIKE
2 — THE DELEGATE
3 — THE ACTIVE MINORITIES
4 — THE GENERAL ASSEMBLY

In the following sequence the members of the film company are seen lying on the ground arguing among themselves. First, a high angle shot shows several of the members sitting beside a tree. The sound of their arguing fades in.

We then see the door of a wooden shed; pinned beneath a sign advertising Pepsi Cola is a page from an Italian newspaper bearing pictures of Stalin and Mao with the words WANTED FOR MURDER daubed around them.

Camera pans rapidly across the members of the team sprawled on the ground in the sunshine.

Close-up of the picture of Stalin, with a red background.

Camera pans slowly across the team, past the sound man holding a microphone boom. A figure walks with the camera in the foreground holding up another copy of the newspaper, with the pictures of Stalin and Mao on the front page.

MAN'S VOICE: *The proposal is a picture of Stalin . . . wanted by the capitalists for murder . . .*

Another shot of the newspaper pinned to the door.

MAN'S VOICE off: *Listen, would you give guns to a clown?*

We see several more members of the film crew sitting on the ground smoking.

Close-up of the head of Stalin against a red background.

MAN'S VOICE off: *When you are saying this is it, you are agreeing with me . . .*

Camera pans across the trees . . .

MAN'S VOICE off: *It's a form of Soviet realism that you are proposing . . .*

Then it tilts down onto the company sprawled on the ground, one of them now holding the newspaper.

MAN'S VOICE off: *Well then, let's get right to the bottom of this line of thinking . . .* The paper is passed from hand to hand. *I say that I'm going even further . . . so we have got to find the right approach . . .*

Another close-up of the newspaper on the shed door, with the words WANTED FOR MURDER. Stalin's face is scored out with heavy black lines, while Mao's face remains untouched beside it. (Still on page 157.)

A shot of the recording engineer sitting on the ground wearing headphones.

MAN'S VOICE off: *Given that the problem — Stalin's picture — is actually in the film.*

The recording engineer points off and the camera pans to show the assistant holding the microphone boom.

SECOND VOICE off: *Don't just say the first thing that comes into your head.*

Resume on the shed door.

FIRST VOICE off: *But the question of the portrayal of Stalin does arise . . .*

We look up at the branches of the trees, silhouetted against the sunny sky; the microphone boom passes briefly across the shot.

FIRST VOICE off: *He is in the film, which means there are differences of opinion, but . . .*

SECOND VOICE off: *Do you feel repressed by this image?*

THIRD VOICE off: *. . . It is difficult to associate easily with Dubceck . . .*

The chattering and argument continue confusedly off.

Close-up of Stalin's image on the red background.

Shot of the recording team with the microphone suspended from its boom in the foreground. Camera pans slightly right.

FOURTH VOICE off: *. . . There, two people with guns in their hands . . .*
Resume on the shed door.

Another shot of the man holding the microphone boom, several other figures seated beyond him.

FIFTH VOICE off: *. . . Because you have no answer to repression . . .*
Resume on the shed door with Stalin and Mao 'wanted for murder'.

SIXTH VOICE off: *. . . Come here, darling, come here, come back . . .*
Resume on several of the company sprawled on the ground.

Camera pans jerkily round in a circle as the speaker is heard over.

SECOND FEMALE VOICE over: *What do we hear? What do we see? Images of people arguing, confused sounds, parts of a poster of Stalin and Mao.*

Shot of the poster on the shed door.

SECOND FEMALE VOICE over: *Why these images? Why these sounds? . . .*

Resume on the film crew, with a stills photographer in the background.

SECOND FEMALE VOICE over: *Why is there an ever-changing relationship between these images and sounds? The intention was to talk about what we experienced in May '68.*

Back to the poster.

SECOND FEMALE VOICE over: *In factories, universities and offices, comrades held meetings and formed organizations.*

We see the stills photographer photographing the scene.

SECOND FEMALE VOICE over: *In spite of confusion during discussions, they still made progress. How can we account for this? How can we discover truth in this confusion? How can we get to the truth correctly?*

Camera pans to show the CAVALRYMAN and UNION DELEGATE in ordinary clothes nearby, taking part in the argument.

SECOND FEMALE VOICE over: *A number of comrades quickly turned to film production. In relation to the rest of the group, they became a minority . . .*

Resume on the poster on the shed door.

SECOND FEMALE VOICE over: *When, after the strike, social democracy, etc. . . .*

A high angled shot of two of the company arguing; one of them gets to his feet.

SECOND FEMALE VOICE over: *. . . became a matter of discussing the general assembly, the comrades immediately came up with a solution . . .*

Close-up of Stalin.

Camera pans in a circle showing people's legs and feet.

SECOND FEMALE VOICE over: *A general assembly should be called immediately, because ultimately that was the best way of discussing it — to arrange a general assembly where the main subject would be the continuation of the film.*

Close-up of Stalin, black bars across his face.

SECOND FEMALE VOICE over: *This meant a discussion of the making of the images and sounds . . .*

Some of the company are seen looking up towards camera.

SECOND FEMALE VOICE over: *. . . which in the film would depict the* *same scenes of the general assembly . . . In May and June '68, the established powers retaliated and repressed these revolutionary groups in France, Italy, Spain and Mexico. The filming of the general assembly was therefore the filming of the general assembly which debated the following sequence, in which the making of images and sounds of this repression is discussed . . .* Camera pans jerkily round the scene again . . . *The editing of the corresponding analyses of this discussion would make it possible to understand the functioning of the general assembly. Which image of repression did the comrades immediately propose? A poster of Stalin and Mao, who are wanted for murder by the capitalists.*

Close-up of the poster again.

SECOND FEMALE VOICE over : *Why Stalin? Because for these comrades, what is usually called the Stalin problem, whether you like it or not, is part of the revolutionary movement.*

A shot of some of the company arguing, a man standing in the foreground. No sound.

Stalin's face on the poster.

Sunlit trees waving in the breeze.

FIRST VOICE off : *How do you explain that?*

SECOND VOICE off : *I'm not saying that he is Stalin, but that others accept him as Stalin . . . One rejects Stalin, but one finds oneself in a Stalinist situation . . . Stalinist, precisely because . . .*

Close-up of Stalin.

We look down on one of the company — the INDIAN — lying on his stomach on the ground, playing with a pebble while the argument rages around him.

THIRD VOICE off : *That's very simple. They've excluded all the characters who were to have been seen in the film.*

FIRST VOICE off : *But we know that.*

SECOND VOICE off : *Consequently, this is a film which collaborates with Papadopoulos.*

THIRD VOICE off : *Thus we take as our image, we take as our image 'Wanted for murder', posted up by Gian Maria Volonte, 'Wanted for murder'.*

Close-up of Stalin.

Resume on the INDIAN lying on the ground; a hand is holding up a board with a picture captioned DZIGA VERTOV on it, hiding the INDIAN's face.

THIRD VOICE off : *And here we should have* ...
> Close-up of Stalin.
> Extreme blurred close-up of the top of the INDIAN's head.

THIRD VOICE off : ... *an image* ...
> Resume on Stalin with black lines daubed across his face.

THIRD VOICE off : ... *which has* ...
> Camera zooms out from close-up of the INDIAN's head.

THIRD VOICE off : ... *not been used before, given the discussion you have just witnessed.*
> A hand holds up a book in front of the camera showing an illustration of Soviet soldiers.

FOURTH VOICE off : *It is extraordinary that* ...
> Close-up of Stalin against the red background.
> Seen from above, the INDIAN's hand fiddles in the dirt on the ground.

FIFTH VOICE off : ... *Party secretary* ...

SECOND VOICE off : *There, for instance, at that place in the film, is something that goes back to Stalin and which we're right up to the neck in — that is realism which ... what is it called now?* ...

ANOTHER VOICE off : *Socialist realism.*

SECOND VOICE off : *Socialist realism.*
> Close-up of Stalin with black bars over his face.

SECOND FEMALE VOICE over : *China* ...
> Resume on the INDIAN's hand playing with a piece of twig.

SECOND FEMALE VOICE over : *The poor farmers of the Kiung-Tsing production brigade meet to denounce the revisionist counter-revolutionary course being taken in the medical and sanitary fields.*
> Shot of the poster.
> The company are seen grouped round a tree, squatting down, sharing out cigarettes.

SECOND FEMALE VOICE over : *Egypt. The workers of the armament factory at Elouan are uniting to demand punishment for the military bureaucrat who is supposed to have collaborated with the Israeli imperialists.*
> Shot of the poster on the shed door.
> Camera tilts up over several more of the company sprawled on the ground, one of them holding a copy of the newspaper with the picture of Mao and Stalin on the front.

SECOND FEMALE VOICE over : *France. Workers at the C.S.F. in Issy-*

les-Moulineaux join forces to denounce the behaviour of one of the permanent representatives of the C.G.T. who has threatened to attack the Marxist-Leninists by name in a pamphlet, thus exposing them to repressive measures by the employer. To see the general assembly only as a debating society is to see it as an abstraction . . . Someone comes into shot and places their hand over the face of Stalin on the newspaper . . . *Because who is speaking and against whom?*

Close-up of Stalin's face covered with black stripes.

Shot of several more of the company, a girl seated in profile in the foreground.

SECOND FEMALE VOICE over : *The original assembly is specific. It reflects the real conflicts of the country, and is itself militant. Who is speaking and against whom?* . . .

Close-up of Stalin against the red background.

We look down on a copy of the newspaper lying beside one of the men's feet. Camera tilts up to show him and others seated on the ground, then right up to trees and sky as the voice continues.

SECOND FEMALE VOICE over : . . . *In China: the masses against a handful of leaders who are attached to the capitalist system. In Egypt: the masses against the military bureaucracy, who are exploiting the people and supported by Russian revisionists.*

Shot of the poster with Stalin ' wanted for murder '.

Resume on the sky again.

SECOND FEMALE VOICE over : *In France: the masses against the French revisionists who are in league with the capitalist exploiters.*

Close-up of Stalin against the red background.

SECOND FEMALE VOICE over : *All people's gatherings are like one another, because the same enemies are met in each country, though in a different manner.*

Camera tilts down over the trees, past the seated company, onto the dusty ground.

SECOND FEMALE VOICE over : *In each country there is the same essential crisis of our times —*

Shot of the poster on the shed door.

SECOND FEMALE VOICE over : *— the crisis of imperialism and modern revisionism* . . .

A shot of the sound engineer with his tape recorder working; a Volkswagen van moves past along a road in the background.

SECOND FEMALE VOICE over : . . . *the era of the united opposition of*

141

*imperialism and modern revisionism against revolutionary movements
. . . Every general assembly held by revolutionaries today . . .*

Close-up of the poster of Stalin and Mao.

SECOND FEMALE VOICE over : *. . . must consider the great problem of
our time —*

Camera tilts down on the company lounging on the ground.

SECOND FEMALE VOICE over : *— the problem of the history of imperialism, the problem of the history of revisionism. And to consider the
problem of the real history of revisionism means in fact to consider
what is usually referred to as the Stalin question. That means no longer
to focus on the image of Stalin, but to try to analyze the classes of
Soviet society, from the beginning of the dictatorship of the proletariat.*

As the commentary ends someone places a black cloth over the
camera lens and the screen goes black.

Then we see a cutting from a French newspaper showing mug
shots of Stalin as a young man from the front and side.

Camera starts moving across the arguing group again.

MALE VOICE : *The most disgusting aspect of the cinema is that the
bourgeoisie and Stalin have the same attitude . . . This is called . . .
This leads to images and sounds of a particular sort being made. This
can be seen in our own practice and right here where nobody feels like
having any fun . . .* Confused shouts of protest.

SECOND MALE VOICE : *Jean-Luc says that within the party this
problem has not been resolved. It's not true . . .*

Close-up of Stalin's face striped with black.

SECOND FEMALE VOICE over : *All the same, it is true . . .*

Resume on the pictures of the young Stalin.

SECOND FEMALE VOICE over : *A badly expressed problem, a wrong
solution.*

Back to his picture on the poster.

SECOND FEMALE VOICE over : *To really put problems forward. Example: to analyze in class terms the practical significance of the speech
of June 23, 1931, about ' New situations, new tasks for the strengthen-
ing of the economy '.*

A brief shot of the sound assistant holding the microphone over
the assembled company.

Back to the drawing of Stalin on the red background.

SECOND FEMALE VOICE over : *Example '37-'38. At the request of Com-*

rade Stalin, Sergei Eisenstein started the shooting of Bezhin Meadow, about the struggle for rural socialization. '37-'38. Spanish Civil War. Together with anarchist militia, the peasant farmers organized an immediate partition of the land. They would be liquidated in the name of the fight against anarchism by the political commissars of the Spanish Communist Party . . .

Camera pans across the arguing group again.

SECOND FEMALE VOICE over: . . . who mechanically applied the directives of the Internationale. To ask the question why is also to ask the question against whom?

MAN standing in foreground: It's always the same. You are anti-Stalin, but you still make Stalinist images.

TITLE black and red letters: IT'S NOT A JUST IMAGE, IT'S JUST AN IMAGE

Close-up of the ' wanted for murder ' poster.

TITLE black and red letters: IT'S NOT A JUST IMAGE, IT'S JUST AN IMAGE

Shot of the poster pinned to the shed door beneath the Pepsi Cola sign.

SECOND FEMALE VOICE over: Stalinist images. Just consider the problem. There is a positive side to everything that has happened: like having shown that an image in itself is nothing, that there is no image outside the context of the class struggle. Having shown this with an image of Stalin. Negative aspect: not having found the right image . . .

TITLE black and red letters: IT'S NOT A JUST IMAGE, IT'S JUST AN IMAGE

The title is diagonally overlaid with the word REPRESSION repeated over and over again.

SECOND FEMALE VOICE over: . . . that is, the necessary and sufficient image.

We see the INDIAN in medium close-up standing beside a waterfall; the CAVALRYMAN's hand, on the left of the shot, is gripping him viciously by the neck. As the voice continues over, the CAVALRYMAN pushes him forward under the waterfall.

SECOND FEMALE VOICE over: Stalin and Mao wanted for murder by *the capitalists — that was a necessary, but inadequate image of repression.*

TITLE black and red letters: IT'S NOT A JUST IMAGE, IT'S JUST AN IMAGE

The title is overlaid with the word REPRESSION as before.

Resume on the INDIAN being doused under the waterfall.

SECOND FEMALE VOICE over: *We must find more images of repression, the only ones we can make at the present.*

MAN'S VOICE over: *Hallo, the laboratories of Humphry Ltd. have refused to develop the film about the dockers on strike, shot by the strikers themselves.*

TITLE black and red letters: REPRE$$ION.

The word RED is superimposed over the two dollar signs.

MAN'S VOICE over: *Three days after the kidnapping of the Yankee ambassador to Brazil the death penalty was restored there.*

Resume on the waterfall. The CAVALRYMAN douses the INDIAN repeatedly under the stream of water.

MAN'S VOICE over: *In Marrakesh, a meeting of progressive students was machine-gunned by a right-wing extremist commando with full government support.*

TITLE black and red letters: REPRE*SS*ION.

The word RED is superimposed over the *SS*.

Resume on the waterfall. The INDIAN stands on the left, the CAVALRYMAN's hand gripping him by the neck.

We now see a YOUTH in a white shirt standing in a field, a hand gripping his shoulder. He is in profile. (Still on page 148.)

TITLE black and red symbols and letters:

1 — THE STRIKE
2 — THE DELEGATE
3 — THE ACTIVE MINORITIES
4 — THE GENERAL ASSEMBLY
5 — REPRESSION
6 — THE ACTIVE STRIKE

Resume on the YOUTH standing in the field, the wind blowing the grass behind him. A man's voice is heard over.

144

NION

COSTRUIRE IL PARTITO IN FABBRIC

WANTED

FOR

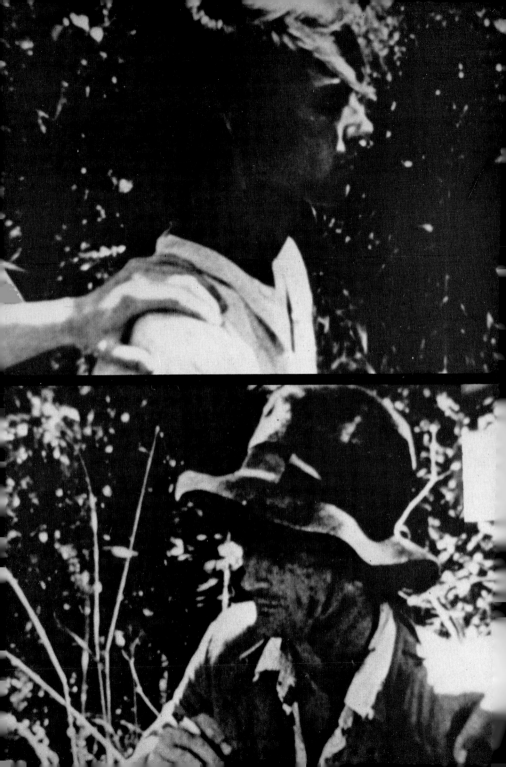

GERARD'S VOICE over: *Marcel, we've been on strike now for four weeks. I'm writing this letter to you, not really knowing if it will reach you, because our comrades at the post office are still on strike, though not for much longer, I think. While the unions are overtly asking for more support for the movement, they are bringing influence to bear in essential sectors so that a majority of the strikers will return to work. And when the post and railway services go back to work, we'll all go back little by little, whether we want to or not. Right?*

Medium close-up of the fugitive YOUNG MAN sitting in the field, smoking a cigarette. His face and clothes are begrimed with blood and dirt; he is wearing a brown felt hat, and there is a hand resting on his shoulder. (Still on page 148.)

GERARD'S VOICE over: *That's clear, anyway, but you know all about that. Being in your situation you'll see things the same as I do. But what can we do to make things change? We've lasted for four weeks and that's a victory for us. Out of 2,000, there are roughly 900 continuing the sit-in in shifts. I say victory, though in fact I don't know how things are with you. Anyway the situation is quite different 500 yards from our factory, at Mazda, Givelaud and Alasef. The first day the official from the C.G.T. told the lads: 'Good, we're stopping work. You go home. When an agreement has been reached, we'll let you know.' Ten or twenty tried to oppose the move and stayed and occupied the factory. But they were deserted by the cowards. At our place 900 took part in the occupation. At the beginning this was enough. About 800 of the lads had worked in the same factory for five or ten years, though they'd never participated before. This and other circumstances made it possible to get a lot of things done and also to start discussions. Everyone who'd taken part in strikes and occupations before said that something had changed. Obviously a lot of them were mainly concerned with playing cards and football and getting off with the women workers. That was another thing that was new — the number of girls that were there. It lasted for three weeks. We discussed things seriously, talked politics, and not only about the demand that the window of the lavatory of workshop 45 should be changed. All this scared the union officials. We also met students. For the strike leaders, though, all this was good. It was they who forced the C.G.T. officials to allow students into the canteen. I must admit this often didn't mean very much, because there were people there speaking a language you just couldn't understand. Some of them used to talk for hours, until everybody got fed up. That's the negative aspect, though. The positive aspect is that these people were part of the fight and were saying some really important things, and that the people coming in from outside prevented the sit-in from weakening. But now, after four weeks, the number of us here has hardly got any bigger.*

Back to the YOUTH, still standing impassively with the hand on his shoulder.

GERARD'S VOICE over: *Last weekend, some of our comrades went home . . .*

Back to the YOUNG MAN sitting in a similar pose.

GERARD'S VOICE over: *And these were people who had been there from the beginning; they went because of their wife, their kids or something else. Well, I suppose that's normal. But in spite of all this, there were still over a hundred people occupying the factory last Saturday and Sunday. People's interest in the ballot was pretty low — cards were very popular. Then I thought of something one of the students had told us . . .*

Back to the YOUTH.

GERARD'S VOICE over: *It seems that at the C.S.F. in Brest, some workers had apparently gone back to work to make transistors by themselves, and had exchanged these with local farmers for vegetables and poultry.*

Resume on the YOUNG MAN.

GERARD'S VOICE over: *His story sounded a bit strange, but when we wanted to know more about it, he got all involved, which shows it's impossible to get any information. He'd called what they were doing in Brest active striking, and said it was the only way to prevent the strike from weakening . . .*

Back to the YOUTH in profile.

GERARD'S VOICE over: *. . . that it was the only way to hit really hard at the employers, the only way to pose concrete problems about power. When I thought of the workshops and the fighting spirit of the people in the workshops, I wondered whether we shouldn't try it as well, just to show that we could keep the factory going ourselves, without the technicians. Our comrades here didn't really know what to make of it. Some agreed with it, while others just said I was dreaming, but they couldn't really say why. That's the situation now. I should be very grateful if you could reply to this letter. Anyway, I hope to see you soon. I'd better close now . . .*

Camera tracks slowly away from the YOUTH and holds on grass and bushes blowing in the wind.

GERARD'S VOICE over: *On Monday, the managers and scabs will be round again, shouting that they want to get back in, in the name of freedom to work.*

Then it tracks further to show the YOUNG MAN sitting on the ground.

GERARD'S VOICE over: *Shit, I hope there'll be enough of us to shut them up. Good-bye.*

We resume on the YOUTH, still standing impassively in profile, and hold on him for some time.

We now see the INDIAN from below, sitting on a fence with a rifle raised in the air, partly obscured by the bushes.

WOMAN'S VOICE over: '*Hello, this is Jean-Pierre Peugeot. Who's speaking?*' — '*Strike committee.*' — '*Listen, young woman. I'm trying to be polite to you. Who are you?*' — '*Strike committee.*' — '*I've told you who I am: Jean-Pierre-Peugeot. Now who are you?*' — '*Strike committee.*' — '*I want to know who I'm talking to.*' — '*Strike committee.*' — '*Jean-Pierre Peugeot here. Are you frightened of saying who you are?*' — '*Strike committee.*'

Resume on the YOUTH in profile, the hand on his shoulder.

MARCEL'S VOICE over: *Gerard, I got your letter. As it happened it came after we'd started work again. We think you're making a mistake. You say that you want to show that you can do without the technicians. You forget that you are not just dealing with a technical division of labour, but with a social-technical division, and you are doing just what the capitalists want you to do if you only work from your own point of view, from your own immediate situation. The Chinese say: you must have a revolution and organize the means of production. Right? They also say: first make the revolution to organize the means of production differently. Even if you managed to organize your active strike so that your lads could go on doing their work, it would still only be a temporary strike, though of a different kind. O.K. I read in the papers that our comrades at Pirelli did the same thing. But it led to nothing more that the loss of fifty million for those in power. We must organize ourselves to fight against the power of the bourgeois state, against its cops, its army which has to attack us to keep us in order — the old order, the same old crap.*

Back to the fugitive YOUNG MAN sitting on the ground, a hand on his shoulder.

TITLE black and red symbols and letters :
1 — THE STRIKE
2 — THE DELEGATE
3 — THE ACTIVE MINORITIES
4 — THE GENERAL ASSEMBLY
5 — REPRESSION
6 — THE ACTIVE STRIKE
7 — THE POLICE STATE

The scene changes to a wide canyon with a stream rushing along through the bottom. It is full of lush greenery with plants growing down the sides. Starting from a high shot of the INDIAN stretched out on a rock with his rifle, camera proceeds to make a series of fast jerky panning movements — to the side, up, down, diagonally — while all the characters seen hitherto dance round and round in a mock battle, the central figure of which is the CAVALRYMAN. They rush to and fro, shouting, falling in the water, picking themselves up again, while the CAVALRYMAN dashes about on his horse, slashing at them with his sabre. We hear the sound of running water as their voices echo across the canyon.

TITLE red letters : DEFEAT⟫⟫→PROVOCATION

The sound of rushing water continues as we see two men — a FRENCHMAN and an AMERICAN — hanging upside down from a tree by the canyon wall. The AMERICAN's responses are in English and as they speak the CAVALRYMAN passes to and fro in the foreground, leading his horse. (Still on page 149.)

FRENCHMAN : *I robbed the First National City Bank — $50,000.*
AMERICAN : *We have done it too.*
FRENCHMAN : *I shot the driver of the Lightedfoot to Heroklod train.*
AMERICAN : *We have done it too.*
FRENCHMAN : *I kidnapped the son of the director of Citroën.*
AMERICAN : *We have done it too.*
FRENCHMAN : *I shot dead the Sheriff of West Berlin.*
AMERICAN : *We have done it too.*
FRENCHMAN : *So we have the same enemies. I'd like to get together with you to find out why we have the same enemies and why we must continue the fight. O.K.?*

156

AMERICAN : *O.K.*

TITLE black and red letters : NEW DEFEAT ⋙→ NEW PROVO-
CATION

The CAVALRYMAN is seen in medium close-up, standing by a wall.
He has got hold of ANNA WIAZEMSKY by the throat and is chok-
ing her, trying to make her talk. Blood is squirted on to her hair
from off-screen; she is back to camera.

CAVALRYMAN in Italian, shaking her : *Talk! Why do you exploit the
sexuality of the proletariat? Why do you give them back in words
what you have already given them back in deeds? Talk! Talk!*

He lets go of her for a moment, then grips her by the throat again
and continues to shout ' *Talk! Talk!* ' intermittently as the commentary continues over.

SECOND FEMALE VOICE over : *A week of struggle. Saturday 17th, the
iron mines of Anderny-Chevillon. Twenty-four-hour strike against the
latest dismissals. Monday 19th, Vendel-Sibelon Ayot. Strike to get a
wage increase of 0.80 francs an hour. Three out of nine blast-furnaces
are shut down.*

CAVALRYMAN over : *Talk! Talk! You are guilty.*

SECOND FEMALE VOICE over : *Tuesday, 20th, the National Institute of
Astronomy and Geophysics. Strike by 150 technicians for job security.
Wednesday 21st, Liquid Air. The steel-workers strike against the in-
trigues of the union officials. Thursday 22nd, Mauduit paper-mill in
Quimper.*

CAVALRYMAN in Italian, shaking WIAZEMSKY : *Talk! Talk! You are
guilty.*

SECOND FEMALE VOICE over : *Provocation through disorder. Insult.
New provocation. New insult . . .* Cut to black *. . . Until their down-
fall. That is the logic of the imperialists and reactionaries of the world.
They'll never be able to change this logic.* Pause. *New strike against
the dismissal of militants.*

Resume on WIAZEMSKY and the CAVALRYMAN, as he continues to
torture her.

CAVALRYMAN in Italian, gripping WIAZEMSKY by the neck : *Talk!
Talk! You're guilty!*

SECOND FEMALE VOICE over : *Friday 23rd, Lycée Bergson, Paris 19.
The Lycée has been closed by the Rector of the Academy of Paris and
plain-clothes police guard the various entrances.*

157

TITLE black and red letters: ANOTHER FIGHT. ANOTHER DE-
FEAT. AND SO TO VICTORY. SUCH IS THE PEOPLE'S
LOGIC.

We now see WIAZEMSKY and the CAVALRYMAN from the reverse
angle. Her face and dress are covered in blood and so is his hand.
He crooks an arm round her neck and slowly begins to strangle
her. She chokes. He continues this, intermittently releasing her
then starting to strangle her again, throughout the following commentary. (Still on page 150.)

SECOND FEMALE VOICE over: *The rashness of revolutionaries has
always been the policeman's best ally. Don't go directly to meeting-
places. Make a detour through a less busy street to make sure you are
not being followed. Write as little as possible. Train yourself to remember addresses. In cases of emergency, remember that a Christian
name is better than a surname, and that an initial is better than a
Christian name. Make appointments over the phone only with small
talk. Don't try to find out what you should not know. Remember that
the enemy is capable of anything. Never be misled when they say: ' We
know everything.' This is never true. Never be tempted by the police
or legal authorities into establishing or re-establishing the truth, which
is an unhealthy habit inculcated by an idealistic bourgeois upbringing.
In this fight there is no truth which is valid for both the exploiters and
their victims.*

WIAZEMSKY claws at the CAVALRYMAN's arm as he chokes her.
Cut to black.

SECOND FEMALE VOICE over: *Fight, defeat. Another fight, another
defeat. Another fight, and so to victory. Such is the people's logic, and
they will never go against this logic.*

Seen in medium close-up, a boy ties a white bandage round WIA-
ZEMSKY's arm.

WIAZEMSKY: *But how shall we recognize one another?*

BOY: *Not only recognize one another, but also let oneself be recog-
nized.*

WIAZEMSKY: *Right. All we have to do is make armbands.*

She starts cutting another band from the boy's shirt with a pair
of scissors. Loud military music.

TITLE: FIGHT. SHOW. 1st MAY.

Seen in high angle medium close-up, WIAZEMSKY ties a bandage round the boy's arm, which is running and glistening with blood.

BOY : *Right. But that's not everything. What colour?*

WIAZEMSKY : *Listen. Look.*

A loud revolutionary song accompanied by guitar, as camera tracks in on the bandage : red blood wells out from underneath it. Cut to black.

Black screen.

SECOND FEMALE VOICE over : *Second part of the film. You have shown a mechanism: the strike, the union official, the general assembly, repression, the police state, etc. You have made a film about a real movement — May '68 in France, '68/'69 in Italy. How did you make it? A little criticism, a little struggle, a little change. Don't forget that it's difficult for any individual to avoid mistakes. Their correction lies in the general movement towards Marxist education. Start again at the beginning, with the people. Be critical of your lack of liaison with the people.*

TITLE black and red symbols and letters :

1 — THE STRIKE

2 — THE DELEGATE

3 — THE ACTIVE MINORITIES

4 — THE GENERAL ASSEMBLY

5 — REPRESSION

6 — THE ACTIVE STRIKE

7 — THE POLICE STATE

LIAISON WITH THE PEOPLE

GODARD over : *To sum up: concentrate, pass on the ideas of the people.*

Long shot of a field of cabbages, a line of electric pylons in the distance.

SECOND FEMALE VOICE over : *It is not enough to have an aim, you've got to solve the problem ...*

We see a farmer backing his horse and cart into a farmhouse.

SECOND FEMALE VOICE over : *... of the methods which will allow you to accomplish this.*

Long shot of a lorry full of farm produce, electric pylons behind. A woman walks round the lorry.

SECOND FEMALE VOICE over : *Your method is wrong. You think that it's enough to quote Mao, to go into the country and film the farm-*

workers and then combine the two to show the necessity of uniting with the rural masses.

A boy and girl are sitting on the ground. The girl smokes while the boy talks. GODARD's voice is dubbed in over.

GODARD over: *The correct formula for the job, for production and for the basic notions of direction. The correct management of every political activity of our party must be based on the following principles.*

A long shot shows grain siloes at a river-side.

SECOND FEMALE VOICE over: *You still talk in slogans, in poster language; you're still apart from the people.*

Two lorries pass one another on a road.

SECOND FEMALE VOICE over: *You're out of step with the others; you're outside the real struggle. Think what your situation really is.*

We look down on an industrial construction site.

SECOND FEMALE VOICE over: *Use the quotations of our Chinese comrades so that they become effective political instruments and not just a ready-made solution. You shout, make predictions, spread opinions, but you don't really investigate.*

A close-up of the boy's face as he talks and laughs, two female hands on his shoulders.

GODARD over: *I've been to the people again, discussing and explaining these words, so that the people can accept, approve and apply them.*

OTHER VOICES over: *To verify the correctness of these ideas in the people's activities.*

GODARD over: *And again, to bring the ideas of the people together and to spread them.*

We look down on a shanty town strewn with rubbish.

SECOND FEMALE VOICE over: *Look here. You say you are analyzing the problem. But you don't make it easy for yourself: you are practising bourgeois sociology, instead of trying to expose the real forces of social class. You use the techniques of cinéma vérité ...*

Another shot of the shanty town, a woman hanging up washing in the foreground.

SECOND FEMALE VOICE over: *You show the misery of the people, but not their struggle. And because you don't show the people struggling, you deny them the means of struggling. Your cinema, your images, your sounds, are those of bourgeois television and its revisionist allies.*

Resume on the boy and the girl sitting on the ground.

GODARD over: *This debate will be continued indefinitely, making the*

ideas we discuss clearer, livelier and more complex. That is the theory.
SECOND FEMALE VOICE over : *Listen. You do more than that. You film blocks of flats and think you are filming people . . .*

Now we see blocks of flats silhouetted against the sky . . .
SECOND FEMALE VOICE over : *You've never even started to consider your real position. You started out making an investigation. But where did you start from? You know that there is no cinema above class, that there is no cinema except that which concerns itself with the class struggle. But what does this mean? It means that the class with the greatest material power, which dominates society, is the one which creates the most significant images both in and with its films. It means that these images are in turn images of its domination. You are involved in the struggle, but who and what are you struggling with today? . . .*

More blocks of flats, a corrugated iron hoarding in the foreground . . .
SECOND FEMALE VOICE over : *You make a film. You make images and sounds. What should you do? You have the means of making films at your disposal . . .*

Two more tower blocks silhouetted against the sky, traffic passing along the road in the foreground . . .
SECOND FEMALE VOICE over : *What is to be done to make images and sounds which do not depict the hegemony of the dominating class? . . .*

A row of tower blocks beneath a cloudy sky, a building site on the right.
SECOND FEMALE VOICE over : *Yes, what can be done? You must not be afraid to know where you are; you must not be afraid to know where you can start. Where are you? You are in France, you are in Italy, in Germany. You are in an imperialist branch of the prevailing imperialism. Where are you? In Prague, in Warsaw and in Berlin, in some revisionist agency of revisionism. If you're not working for Brezhnev Studios-Mosfilm, you are working for Nixon-Paramount. It means that ultimately you are always doing the same thing, because when you work for Brezhnev-Mosfilm, you are in fact being a lackey to the other master, Nixon-Paramount.*

Long shot of an open industrial site, some men and a tractor in the centre of shot.
SECOND FEMALE VOICE over : *You forget that this master has been demanding the same film for fifty years. You forget that this film has*

one name — the Western — and that this is not by chance.

Cars pass in front of a warehouse outside which stands a mobile crane, with a large section of piping suspended from its arm.

SECOND FEMALE VOICE over: *You start your investigation and you learn that your methods are partly influenced by the dominant ideology. Don't get your primary tasks and secondary tasks confused. Though it only lasts the duration of one sequence, in this film the principal task is theory. Hollywood. Producers. Manufacturers. Factory.*

TITLE blue and red symbols and letters:

1 — THE STRIKE
2 — THE DELEGATE
3 — THE ACTIVE MINORITIES
4 — THE GENERAL ASSEMBLY
5 — REPRESSION
6 — THE ACTIVE STRIKE
7 — THE POLICE STATE
THE A THEORY

Low angle shot of trees silhouetted against a sunlit sky.

SECOND FEMALE VOICE over: *Hollywood shows this in the form of cinema, as something wonderful, dreamlike, for which you have to pay admission. But this dream is also a weapon in Hollywood's hands.*

We are looking down a pathway with high trees and shrubs on either side. As the voice continues over, the CAVALRYMAN appears riding towards us on his horse, towing the INDIAN behind him with a rope fixed round his neck.

SECOND FEMALE VOICE over: *Hollywood wants to make you believe that this dream is reality, that it is more real than reality itself. Hollywood is trying to fool you, and will use any means to achieve its ends. Hollywood tries to make you believe that the image of a horse is really a horse and that this image of a horse is even more real than a horse, which it isn't to begin with. Hollywood makes you believe that this movie Indian is more real than an Indian and that the extra on horseback is more real than a Union soldier.*

Western style music. Camera pans right as the CAVALRYMAN leaves the path and drags the INDIAN off into the trees.

Resume on the beginning of the shot as the CAVALRYMAN rides into view again and the process is repeated.

SECOND FEMALE VOICE over: *This extra is called an actor. This actor is called a character. The adventures of these characters are called a film and the making of this film is called direction. To this end, all means are acceptable: costumes, make-up, disguises, performances. Every year Hollywood decorates and rewards the best producers in the world and the game goes on. The imperialist representation of reality comes face to face with reality itself. The Moscow Film Festival. The Pesaro Film Festival. The Leipzig Film Festival.*

High angle shot of another road. Camera pans as the CAVALRY-MAN rides past, towing the INDIAN behind him and shouting. (Still on page 150.)

CAVALRYMAN in Italian : *I am General Motor!*

INDIAN : *I am black! I am an Indian!*

CAVALRYMAN simultaneously, in Italian : *I am General Motor! I am General Motor!*

They go off up the road.

SECOND FEMALE VOICE over : *What is being done in the Brezhnev-Mosfilm zone of influence?*

Camera tilts upwards over trees and sky. As the speaker continues the camera scans the treetops in a circular motion and then tilts down towards the ground.

SECOND FEMALE VOICE over : *What kind of films are being made in Algiers? What kind in Havana? There is a struggle against Nixon-Paramount but what is really going on? The progressive cinema has naturally understood that a film is the relationship between images and sounds. But is the progressive cinema examining this relationship seriously? Where does this relationship come from? How does it work? From whom? For whom? And against whom?*

Resume on the previous shot as the CAVALRYMAN tows the INDIAN up the road again. The panning movement is repeated as they pass.

SECOND FEMALE VOICE over : *No, the progressive cinema does not ask itself these questions. Why does it refuse to ask them in class terms? Sometimes it modifies a sound, sometimes an image. The progressive cinema then imagines that it is creating new relationships, but it is mistaking quantity for quality, and these relationships are only abstractedly modified. Brezhnev-Mosfilm claims that it is attacking Nixon-Paramount, but in reality it is supporting it.*

We look across a field to a grassy bank. The CAVALRYMAN appears in the distance, towing the INDIAN behind him, and camera pans as they pass by and go up a slope between some trees. The CAVALRYMAN is declaiming in Italian, the INDIAN in English as he reads from a book.

SECOND FEMALE VOICE over: *Underground London, Paris, Amsterdam, New York* ...

Resume on the beginning of the shot; the process is repeated.

SECOND FEMALE VOICE over: *Here is a cinema which thinks it is liberated. A sound which thinks it is liberating an image. A cinema which thinks it is liberated. A drug cinema. A sex cinema. A cinema which claims it has been liberated by poetry, art. A cinema without taboos, except against the class struggle. A class cinema. The flunkey of Nixon-Paramount, the flunkey of imperialism.*

GLAUBER ROCHA is seen standing at a crossroads with arms outstretched, pointing in opposite directions. He is singing the ballad from *Antonio das Mortes*.

SECOND FEMALE VOICE over: *You mentioned at the beginning a road laid out by the history of the revolutionary movement. But where is it? In front of us? Behind us? Left? Right? And how? You have changed your method. You asked the cinema of the Third World where it was* ...

A pregnant girl with a bag slung over her shoulder and wearing red shoes comes up the road behind Rocha and stops in front of him. (Still on page 151.)

GIRL to ROCHA: *I beg your pardon for disturbing you in your class struggle. I know it is very important. But which is the way to the political film?*

ROCHA points to the left and says: *That way is the unknown cinema, the cinema of adventure.* He points behind him to the right: *That way the Third World cinema, a dangerous cinema — divine, marvellous.*

As he continues speaking the girl walks up the track to the right, to where a red ball is lying on the ground some yards away. She kicks the ball away, then comes back towards ROCHA; the ball rolls slowly down the track after her.

ROCHA: *A cinema of the oppression of imperialist consumption is a dangerous, divine, marvellous cinema, a cinema out to repress the fascist oppression of terrorism.*

SECOND FEMALE VOICE over: *And there you discovered the really intricate aspects of the struggle. You discovered that you do not have the means of analyzing it.*

164

ROCHA: *It is a dangerous, divine marvellous cinema.*

Camera pans left, losing ROCHA, as the girl goes behind him and disappears into some trees.

ROCHA off: *It is a cinema that will build everything — technique, projection rooms, distribution, technicians, 300 movie makers to make 600 films a year for the entire Third World. It's the cinema of technology, it's for the people, to spell it out to the masses of the Third World. It is cinema.*

SECOND FEMALE VOICE over: *You're back to the concrete situation. In Italy, France, Germany, in Warsaw, in Prague, you have seen that the materialist film emerges only when it confronts the bourgeois conception of performance, representation, in terms of the class struggle.* Cut to black. *Struggle against the bourgeois notion of representation.*

A shot of plants and flowers waving in the breeze.

SECOND FEMALE VOICE over: *Struggle against the bourgeois notion of representation. Cut to black.*

A high angle shot shows the GIRL in the pink dress sitting on the ground beside some bushes, gazing at a flower.

SECOND FEMALE VOICE over: *Yes. In order to wrest the means of production from imperialist hands, in order to wrest ideological domination from their hands. The bourgeoisie talks about representation. But what does it mean by that? Cut to black.*

We see a shot of the sound man in the film crew standing in a field; in the background is a river and a waterfall. The sound man has his tape recorder slung from his neck and the microphone boom balanced across his shoulders, and there is a cine camera standing on the ground in front of him.

SECOND FEMALE VOICE over: *In ten seconds you will be looking at a character on a bourgeois film screen. He is a Western character from a psychological drama, a thriller, a historical film. It doesn't make any difference. In fact he's always the seducer. He describes the room where you are sitting.*

High angle close-up of an Italian sitting next to a waterfall. He is talking directly towards camera, gesticulating at the audience. The voice over interprets.

SECOND FEMALE VOICE over: *He says he is in the dark . . . He says there are more people in the balcony . . . He says there's an old man sitting in the fifth row . . . He says there's a good looking girl at the back . . . He says he'd like to lay her. He'd like to give her flowers*

He asks her to join him on the screen . . . There's lots of green . . . The air is clear . . .

Camera zooms back to show him from a high angle, standing by the waterfall.

SECOND FEMALE VOICE over: '*Don't you believe it?' he says. 'Then come here, you bunch of turds!' . . . Wonderful summer's day . . . Sunshine. Truth.*

Resume on the picture of the sound engineer.

SECOND FEMALE VOICE over: *Struggle against the bourgeois notion of representation. Wrest the means of production from the hands of the dominant ideology. That is the most we can do. The most is to be able to say: this image is red.*

We look down on an expanse of green undergrowth waving in the breeze.

SECOND FEMALE VOICE over: *Red. Red. Without a workers' and peasants' triple alliance with the military, the least we can do, the least, is to spell it out. To know how to learn.*

A shot of the word EDUCATION chalked in pink and white chalk on a blackboard.

SECOND FEMALE VOICE over: *And for you, to know how to learn means looking the whole bitter, absurd, dirty spectacle in the face.*

Medium close-up of the UNION DELEGATE standing amid greenery, reading from Waldeck-Rochet.

SECOND FEMALE VOICE over: *The spectacle of the revisionist school teacher, who collaborates with the supporters of the ideological domination of the bourgeoisie.*

Resume on the shot of EDUCATION chalked on the blackboard, then cut to black.

The UNION DELEGATE and ANNA WIAZEMSKY are seen standing in a field, each behind a folding table. On the one in front of WIAZEMSKY is a pile of books.

UNION DELEGATE in Italian: *The Communist Party has decided to give the people culture. Miss Althusser, what people have we got here?*

WIAZEMSKY: *First, the people of the Third World.*

UNION DELEGATE in Italian: *Let the people of the Third World come forward.*

WIAZEMSKY clapping her hands: *Will the people of the Third World come forward please.* She hands the DELEGATE a book.

UNION DELEGATE in Italian, looking at it then handing it back: *No*

. . . He rejects another one . . . *No* . . .

He takes another book from WIAZEMSKY as the INDIAN comes into shot; camera tracks slightly, losing her, as she motions the INDIAN to one side of the DELEGATE's table.

UNION DELEGATE in Italian, reading the title : '*How to read* Das Kapital'. *Good.* Writing a dedication in the book : *In friendship and regard for the inhabitants of the Third World!* He hands it to the INDIAN, then stops him as he is about to go off. *One moment. Start at chapter two.*

The INDIAN puts a piece of meat between the pages and bites into it like a sandwich as he goes off. Camera moves with him showing another table, beside which is piled an assortment of weaponry including a machine-gun and two or three rifles. (Still on page 151.)

SECOND FEMALE VOICE over : *What did the revisionist schoolteacher just say? He said: 'Read* Das Kapital'. *He did not ask you to use it. Use it. He criticizes the defects of the people, but he does not do this from the people's point of view. By treating a comrade like you treat an enemy, he has taken the position of the enemy.*

TITLE red letters : COMBAT

Sound of a flute being played inexpertly off.

Resume on the scene. The UNION DELEGATE and WIAZEMSKY have disappeared. A rifle lies beside the books on WIAZEMSKY's table. A STUDENT, similarly dressed to the YOUNG MAN seen earlier, comes into view and dances round the tables, blowing on a recorder.

STUDENT : *I learnt to play music; good, isn't it?*

VOICES off shouting in protest : *It's disgusting! . . . It's shit! . . . It's horrible! . . .*

STUDENT : *Don't you like it? Isn't it nice?*

VOICES off : *Really horrible! . . . It's piss awful! . . .*

STUDENT : *Now wait a minute! . . .*

VOICES off : *Shut up! . . . Belt up! . . .*

STUDENT : *Don't you like it? . . .*

VOICES off : *Wrap up! . . .*

He sits on the edge of WIAZEMSKY's table.

STUDENT : *I think I play rather well. Don't you like it? You must like it.* Giving up as the others protest loudly : *O.K., O.K.*

167

Discouraged, he picks up the rifle from the table and walks off to the left.

TITLE black letters : CRITICISM

Resume on the scene. The STUDENT reappears from the left, carrying the rifle and recorder, and sits down on the edge of the table.

VOICE off : *Did you take part in the class struggle?*

STUDENT : *Yes, I was at Cléon.*

VOICE off : *Were you at Strasbourg?*

STUDENT : *Yes.*

VOICE off : *Were you at Sochaux?*

STUDENT : *Yes.*

VOICES off : *Were you in South America? . . . Were you at Battipaglia?*

STUDENT : *I was at Battipaglia. I did my self-criticism.*

VOICES off : *Were you at La Paz? Did you take part in the demonstration against the visit of Rockefeller?*

STUDENT : *Yes, I did that too. I did my self-criticism, took part in the class struggle and learnt to play music.*

VOICES off : *Were you at the May celebrations in Madrid which had been forbidden by Franco?*

STUDENT : *Yes, I was at the May celebrations in Madrid which had been forbidden by Franco. I learnt to play music there too.*

VOICES off : *And what did you play there?*

STUDENT : *Listen.* He starts to play the tune of ' Il était un petit navire '.

TITLE red letters : COMBAT

Resume on the scene. The STUDENT makes a mistake and stops.

STUDENT : *That's not quite right, is it?*

VOICE off : *No, it's not quite right.*

STUDENT : *Maybe I should go on. I'll go on with the class struggle and finish my self-criticism. It'll be better afterwards.* He gets up and starts to go off.

TITLE red letters : TRANSFORMATION

We now see the fugitive YOUNG MAN seated on one of the tables minus his jacket; his head is thrown back and his face is covered in blood, which has run down onto his shirt and trousers. The CAVALRYMAN stands over him with his rifle and issues a command to the UNION DELEGATE, who appears from the left and starts to examine him. He puts his ear to the YOUNG MAN's back, listening for his heart (Still on page 152), then tries his pulse, and finally — apparently finding him dead — closes his eyes. He lifts the YOUNG MAN's leg and pats him on the knee, chatting to the CAVALRYMAN meanwhile.

SECOND FEMALE VOICE over: *Class medicine. France. Text from a medical school handbook on industrial medicine prepared for fifth-year students: 'The fatigue index is less related to objective criteria than to subjective or personality factors. The departmental chief and the foreman are in the best position for observation and for a regular investigation into fatigue. They are direct witnesses to diminishing performances and a lowering of the production rate. The most important task for the doctor is to discover the origins of this fatigue . . .'*

The CAVALRYMAN and the UNION DELEGATE go off and camera tracks in on the YOUNG MAN, whose head flops forward, lifeless.

SECOND FEMALE VOICE over: *'The medical student therefore learns that he must work hand in hand with the foreman and he thus becomes in a way the other's scientific alter ego.'*

TITLE red and black letters: COMBAT — CRITICISM — TRANSFORMATION

SECOND FEMALE VOICE over: *There is clear division of labour for these guardian angels of capitalism: the foreman searches out the ills, while the doctor cures them. Both play the same role in the social division of labour. Surveillance and repression.*

The YOUNG MAN is seen in medium close-up. A pair of woman's hands appear holding a clean white cloth, raise the YOUNG MAN's head and wipe the blood from his face.

SECOND FEMALE VOICE over: *People's medicine. China. The transformation of the medical and sanitary system is an important part in the transformation of the social superstructure. After the founding of the new China . . . the new China . . . a series of provisions were made to ensure medical care and hygienic assistance for the rural population. The workers' health improved considerably, but Lio-Tsa-Tsji, that eternal renegade, took the revisionist way in medicine and health care. He wanted to centralize the service in the cities. He entered into the erroneous theory of hospitals that would be worthy of the name.*

TITLE red letters: TRANSFORMATION

169

TITLE red letters : COMBAT

SECOND FEMALE VOICE over : *The lack of doctors and pharmaceutical products in rural areas was one of the reasons why it took China so long to free itself from the legacy of the past.*

Resume on the YOUNG MAN. The woman's hands now smooth his hair down and methodically smear the remaining blood evenly across his face.

SECOND FEMALE VOICE over : *The great cultural revolution of the proletariat broke up this revisionist counter-revolutionary tendency. The poor and semi-poor peasants took the medical health system into their own hands. They have set up medical laboratories and they run ambulance services. Thus the rural areas achieved great improvements in the field of medical health. The seventy-nine production groups in the commune of Yong Fang, in the Nanking district, have a number of these communal medical workers at their disposal. Minor wounds and illnesses are dealt with within each group, while minor operations are carried out in the commune. A co-operative system has begun to be enforced. Poor and semi-poor peasants are ensured immediate treatment.*

TITLE black and red letters : COMBAT — CRITICISM

A high angle medium close-up shows the GIRL in the pink bustle dress seen previously, sitting in a meadow reading from a book.

GIRL reading : '*Les Beaux Quartiers*', *by Marcel Proust, page 145.*

SECOND FEMALE VOICE over : *Death to bourgeois culture!*

A hand appears from the right holding a sickle and takes a swing at the GIRL's neck. At the same time another hand swings a hammer down towards her head. (Still on page 152.)

GIRL reading : '*I have never been able to remember the room which gave on to the street . . .*'

The hands swing the hammer and sickle down again, halt a few inches from the GIRL's head and neck, and then withdraw.

SECOND FEMALE VOICE over : *Death to bourgeois culture!*

GIRL reading : '*That means that there exists only one way of speaking. Once in the hotel, there was nothing left, no embankment, no . . .*'

The hands swing the hammer and sickle again.

SECOND FEMALE VOICE over : *Death to bourgeois culture!*

GIRL reading : '. . . *not even the San Marco canal, the crowd and the pigeons . . .'*

The hands swing the hammer and sickle again.

SECOND FEMALE VOICE over : *Death to bourgeois culture!*

GIRL reading : '. . . *the sun in the distance on San Giorgio Maggiore. That was a world in itself, by itself . . .'*

The hands swing the hammer and sickle again.

SECOND FEMALE VOICE over : *Death to bourgeois culture!*

GIRL reading : '. . . *and for itself, as they say. The steps, the passages . . .'*

The hands swing the hammer and sickle again.

SECOND FEMALE VOICE over : *Death to bourgeois culture!*

GIRL reading : '. . . *the dreary walls of the entire upper part of the room in darkness . . . Because of the lamps, one loses . . .'*

The hands swing the hammer and sickle again.

SECOND FEMALE VOICE over : *Death to bourgeois culture!*

A high angle shot of the INDIAN lying on the ground reading *Das Kapital* in Italian.

SECOND FEMALE VOICE over : *The revolutionary doesn't listen to the revisionist schoolteacher. He doesn't start from the second chapter. He starts from the first chapter of* Das Kapital *by Karl Marx. He reads how to use it. 'The wealth of societies in which capitalist methods of production are found is made up of a gigantic collection of goods. In the first place, these goods exist as external objects, of which the qualities will satisfy human needs of one sort or another. In capitalist society the utility value of the goods is at the same time the material basis of an exchange value.'*

Resume on the GIRL in the field, reading.

GIRL reading : *' Things and words '* . . .

The hands swing the hammer and sickle again.

SECOND FEMALE VOICE over : *Open fire on the revisionist intellectual who is the unwitting ally of bourgeois culture.*

GIRL reading : . . . *by Laurent Leroy, Central Committee of the Communist Party in France.*

The hands swing the hammer and sickle again.

SECOND FEMALE VOICE over : *Open fire on the revisionist intellectual who is the unwitting ally of bourgeois culture.*

GIRL reading : *' Throughout the mercantile experience, the control of wealth is made up of the same . . .'*

The hands swing the hammer and sickle again.

171

SECOND FEMALE VOICE over : *Death, fire, death.*

Resume on the INDIAN lying on the ground, reading *Das Kapital.* Close-up of his face daubed in greasepaint as seen near the beginning of the film, his hand thrown up over his forehead.

SECOND FEMALE VOICE over : *The theory of Marx — Engels — Lenin has universal value. It should not be considered as dogma but as a guide to action.*

FIRST FEMALE VOICE over : *In France, for instance, young workers in a provincial technical training centre threw out the representative of the Maréchal factories who had come to supervise the examinations.*

Resume on the INDIAN lying on the ground.

SECOND FEMALE VOICE over : *You must not be satisfied with learning Marxist-Leninist terminology; Marxist-Leninism has to be learnt as the science of revolution. It is not enough only to study the general laws set down by Marx, Lenin and Engels, based on their extensive studies of life and revolutionary experience. You must also examine the methods and arguments they use in studying and solving problems.*

Resume on the face covered in greasepaint.

MAN'S VOICE over : *In Italy, for instance, the inhabitants of a small town occupied the town hall, stopped the trains and built barricades, because they had been without water and electricity for three days after their refusal to pay higher rates.*

SECOND FEMALE VOICE over : *You must be able to arm yourself with self-criticism.*

TITLE red and black letters : COMBAT — CRITICISM

We then return to the two tables standing in the field. The GIRL in the pink dress can just be seen beyond them, seated on the ground. ANNA WIAZEMSKY appears on the left and stands behind the other table, which has nothing on it. Holding a piece of paper, she addresses the camera.

WIAZEMSKY : *Less than ten minutes ago, comrades, I wanted to educate the Third World; and now I have done my self-criticism. She reads: 'Paragraph 1: . . . And what was the university in the past? The university has frequently been called a kindergarten for adults. It is true that the majority of those who went to university . . .'* Shouts of protest off. *Quiet! . . .*

VOICE off : *That's self-criticism.*

WIAZEMSKY : *'. . . went there because people sent them there and be-*

172

cause people wanted to send them there . . .' Loud shouts of protest. *I'm doing my self-criticism. Let me continue.* She continues, shouting : *'Paragraph 2: . . . And what were the contents of . . .'*

The STUDENT runs in from the left and stands behind the table with the books on it. He picks up a book and shouts straight at the audience, while WIAZEMSKY continues screaming her self-criticism and the protest group shout and jeer off-screen.

STUDENT : *Hurrah for the class struggle. Comrades, I come from Fiat. Fiat is my university. The comrades wrote a pamphlet. With 'Poter Operario' and 'Commissione Liceo Gioberti', we started to put a pamphlet together.*

WIAZEMSKY throws her text down on the table in disgust, while the STUDENT continues to shout, referring to the book he is holding.

STUDENT : *We ask five questions.* In Italian : *'What do you think about your work?'*

VOICE off, in Italian : *Strike!*

STUDENT in Italian : *'What are your demands?'*

SHOUTS off, in Italian : *Revolution!*

STUDENT in Italian : *'Which struggle and organization do you consider to be the most meaningful?'*

SHOUTS off, in Italian : *Strike!*

STUDENT in Italian : *'What help can the student movement give to the workers' struggle?'*

SHOUTS off, in Italian : *Strike!*

STUDENT in Italian : *'Do you think it would be useful to form a massive united organization of students and young workers?'* More loud shouts off. The STUDENT looks at his watch and says, in French : *It's time I went. I've got a class at Pirelli's. We have practical tasks at Pirelli — they have occupied the factory; I'm going there now.*

He goes off, while WIAZEMSKY picks up another book from the table and starts to declaim from it. Her voice is drowned as the YOUNG MAN with the blood-covered face and the INDIAN file past her loudly chanting '*Strike*' in Italian, carrying a pick and a shovel. She continues to read, raising her left fist in the air, while the commentary begins again.

SECOND FEMALE VOICE over : *It is time that teaching is revealed to the masses as a weapon in the hands of the bourgeoisie. The number of those who will tolerate their role as victims and accomplices will con-*

173

*sistently grow smaller. The camouflage no longer hides anything —
neither the nature of our society nor the special place reserved for
those who go to college to become servants of the bourgeoisie . . . ' A
sinecure and a status in the comfortable propriety of the bourgeoisie.'*

WIAZEMSKY reaches the end of her discourse, throws the book
down on the table and sings loudly with the others in chorus off-
screen.

TITLE black and red symbols and letters :

1 — THE STRIKE
2 — THE DELEGATE
3 — THE ACTIVE MINORITIES
4 — THE GENERAL ASSEMBLY
5 — REPRESSION
6 — THE ACTIVE STRIKE
7 — THE POLICE STATE
THE WORKER DIRECTED FACTORY

Cut to black as the commentary is heard.

SECOND FEMALE VOICE over : *Good, you have developed your theory.
Get rid of illiteracy. You have seen that this too was another front in
the battle. Good. Now back to practical things. France, May-June '68.
For a number of months there was only one word: ' autonomy '. This
word has a dark and confusing history. Turin '19. Barcelona '37. A
week in Budapest '56. A red glow fills the screen. You have been theo-
rizing again. You began in May. Tell me about autonomy. Try and
find the right words.*

The complete film company are seen from a high angle lying in a
meadow, debating. They are all talking at once and only a few
sentences are distinguishable in the general confusion. The picture has been scratched almost beyond recognition and has been
overlaid with circles and strips of film shining translucently.

VOICES out of the confused noise : *But you don't know how to do it
. . . The idea of writing a play about autonomy . . . There were people
there, then a group of workers arrived . . . The bourgeoisie . . . and
. . . and the active revolutionary minorities and the people who were
going to advise on the subject of autonomy in the play . . .*

The screen goes red again.

SECOND FEMALE VOICE over : *Look, you surely don't think they are the
right terms. They're even more abstract than before. Just think. The*

concrete situation. Autonomy. Example: Yugoslavia.

Resume on the film company seen through the half obliterated film. More talking and confused shouting.

VOICE : *We must applaud here.*

Red screen.

SECOND FEMALE VOICE over : *The restoration of the capitalist system in Yugoslavia* . . .

Resume on the mutilated picture of the film company. Camera pans across the scene.

CONFUSED SOUND OF VOICES.

Red screen.

SECOND FEMALE VOICE over : . . . *came into being because public enterprise* . . .

Back to the film company.

CONFUSED SOUND OF VOICES.

Red screen.

SECOND FEMALE VOICE over : . . . *which played an important part in the Yugoslav economy* . . .

Film company, mutilated film.

CONFUSED SOUND OF VOICES.

Red screen.

SECOND FEMALE VOICE over : . . . *changed and degenerated.*

Film company, mutilated film.

CONFUSED SOUND OF VOICES.

Red screen.

SECOND FEMALE VOICE over : *The economy of the workers' self-government is a special kind of state capitalism.*

Film company, mutilated film.

CONFUSED SOUND OF VOICES.

Red screen.

SECOND FEMALE VOICE over : *This state capitalism* . . .

Film company, mutilated film.

CONFUSED SOUND OF VOICES.

Red screen.

SECOND FEMALE VOICE over : . . . *is not that which exists for the needs of the proletariat.*

Film company, mutilated film.

CONFUSED SOUND OF VOICES.

Red screen.

SECOND FEMALE VOICE over : *It is a variety of state capitalism . . .*
Film company, mutilated film.
CONFUSED SOUND OF VOICES.
Red screen.
SECOND FEMALE VOICE over : *. . . which exists because of completely different conditions . . .*
Film company, mutilated film.
CONFUSED SOUND OF VOICES.
Red screen.
SECOND FEMALE VOICE over : *. . . caused by the degeneration of the dictatorship of the proletariat.*
Film company, mutilated film. Camera pans across the scene.
CONFUSED SOUND OF VOICES.
Red screen.
SECOND FEMALE VOICE over : *Since 1950, Tito's clique has passed a series of resolutions and laws which are intended to bring about autonomy of the workers in factories, mines, the communications media, commerce, agriculture, public works and all other state enterprises. The application of this concept of self-government by the workers consists of placing enterprises under the control of the workers' collectives. These collectives buy their own raw materials, decide which goods they are going to make, in what quantity, and what their price shall be; they sell their products on the market, fix the wages and decide on the division of the profits.*
Film company, mutilated film.
CONFUSED SOUND OF VOICES.
Red screen.
SECOND FEMALE VOICE over : *From a theoretical point of view, everyone knows — no matter how little their knowledge of Marxism — that concepts such as 'worker autonomy' and 'workers' factories' have never been Marxist concepts, but ideas put forward by anarcho-syndicalists and bourgeois socialists. In the Communist Manifesto, Marx and Engels say: 'The proletariat will make use of its political superiority to wrest all monetary power from the hands of the bourgeoisie and to place all the means of production in the hands of the state.' This is a fundamental socialist principle. Just after the October Revolution, when a number of people wanted to hand over the factories to the old producers so that they could organize production again, Lenin criticized them, saying that this would lead to a reaction against the dic-*

176

tatorship of the proletariat.

Film company, mutilated film.

CONFUSED SOUND OF VOICES.

Red screen.

SECOND FEMALE VOICE over : *For all these reasons . . .*

Film company, mutilated film.

CONFUSED SOUND OF VOICES.

Red screen.

SECOND FEMALE VOICE over : *. . . the 'worker autonomy' initiated by the Tito clique . . .*

Film company, mutilated film.

CONFUSED SOUND OF VOICES.

Red screen.

SECOND FEMALE VOICE over : *. . . has acted in such a way that public enterprise is totally removed from the orbit of socialist economy.*

Film company, mutilated film. Camera pans across the scene.

CONFUSED SOUND OF VOICES.

Red screen.

SECOND FEMALE VOICE over : *The main symptoms of this phenomenon are: . . .*

Film company, mutilated film.

CONFUSED SOUND OF VOICES.

Red screen.

SECOND FEMALE VOICE over : *1. Suppression of unified State economic planning.*

Film company, mutilated film.

CONFUSED SOUND OF VOICES.

Red screen.

SECOND FEMALE VOICE over : *2. Profit is considered to be the main incentive of the enterprise's programme.*

Film company, mutilated film.

CONFUSED SOUND OF VOICES.

Red screen.

SECOND FEMALE VOICE over : *Production policy is decided by the workers . . .*

Film company, non-mutilated film. They are all sitting in a field. The microphone boom can be seen in the centre, a white parasol in the background.

CONFUSED SOUND OF VOICES.

Red screen.

SECOND FEMALE VOICE over: *. . . but it is not geared to satisfy the needs of society . . .*

Film company, mutilated film. The effect is caused by strips of movie film laid over the image in all directions.

CONFUSED SOUND OF VOICES.

Red screen.

SECOND FEMALE VOICE over: *. . . and is lagging behind in this respect. The main motive is to make profits, as in capitalist enterprises.*

Film company, mutilated film.

CONFUSED SOUND OF VOICES.

Red screen.

SECOND FEMALE VOICE over: *3. Favouring a policy which encourages capitalistic free trade.*

Film company, mutilated film.

CONFUSED SOUND OF VOICES.

Red screen.

SECOND FEMALE VOICE over: *4. The use of credit in banking to support capitalistic free trade.*

Film company, mutilated film.

CONFUSED SOUND OF VOICES.

Red screen.

SECOND FEMALE VOICE over: *Loans are given to those who can pay back in the shortest possible time . . .*

Film company, mutilated film.

CONFUSED SOUND OF VOICES.

Red screen.

SECOND FEMALE VOICE over: *. . . and the rate of interest is high.*

Film company, mutilated film.

CONFUSED SOUND OF VOICES.

Red screen.

SECOND FEMALE VOICE over: *5. The relations between the various enterprises . . .*

Film company, mutilated film.

CONFUSED SOUND OF VOICES.

Red screen.

SECOND FEMALE VOICE over: *. . . are not the socialist bonds of mutual assistance, but the capitalist and competitive bonds of a so-called free market.*

TITLE black and red symbols and letters :
        1 — THE STRIKE
        2 — THE DELEGATE
        3 — THE ACTIVE MINORITIES
        4 — THE GENERAL ASSEMBLY
        5 — REPRESSION
        6 — THE ACTIVE STRIKE
        7 — THE POLICE STATE
        THE WORKER DIRECTED FACTORY

SECOND FEMALE VOICE over : *You see that your previous ideas are still confused. If you go on like that, you'll end the film by saying that socialism is a bed of roses.*
    Close-up of ANNA WIAZEMSKY with poppies in her hair, sitting on the ground, eating a large French sandwich. As the commentary continues she chews on the sandwich, looking straight at camera.
SECOND FEMALE VOICE over : *It is quite true that theory becomes a material force once it reaches the people. But you've got to have valid ideas. Think about the concrete situation.*
    Close-up of a mirror held in WIAZEMSKY's hands, her face reflected in it.
SECOND FEMALE VOICE over : *Think your theories over again. Example: the invention of photography.*

TITLE red and black symbols and letters :
        1 — THE STRIKE
        2 — THE DELEGATE
        3 — THE ACTIVE MINORITIES
        4 — THE GENERAL ASSEMBLY
        5 — REPRESSION
        6 — THE ACTIVE STRIKE
        7 — THE POLICE STATE
        THE B THEORY

    Resume on the image of WIAZEMSKY in the mirror.
SECOND FEMALE VOICE over : *The invention of photography. For whom? Against whom? For whom? Against whom? For whom? France. Louis Philippe. The bank. Investment. The beginning of the industrial revolution.*
    We follow the GIRL in the pink bustle dress as she walks across the

179

screen, turning in a circle, filming the scenery around her with a cine-camera.

SECOND FEMALE VOICE over: *Accelerated growth of the proletariat. Class struggle. The necessity of changing the dominant ideology. Class struggle. The necessity of finding new methods. Class struggle. Photography forces literature and painting into the background. Against whom? Against the people in their struggle. Photography. For the bourgeoisie, two functions: 1. Identification of class enemies. 2. Disguising reality.*

We follow an actor with a gun as he rushes through a stream and off to the left, while another man follows him taking photographs.

SECOND FEMALE VOICE over: *1. In 1897 the police in Versailles photographed a number of people at a protest gathering. 2. In 1871, photographs of shot* communards *appeared in bourgeois newspapers . . . Today: Paris Match/Vietnam . . .* Cut to black *. . . Newsweek/Palestine; L'Espresso/Brazil.*

Seen from above, the INDIAN is crouched on a bank beside a stream, a rifle stuck upright in the water, while behind him several guns are laid out on a blanket. He examines a pistol, puts it down, then picks up a camera and inspects it with interest. Sound of running water.

SECOND FEMALE VOICE over: *Fight the bourgeois concept of representation. Wrest the control of the cinema, photography and television from the hands of the controlling ideology. Don't represent the problem in an abstract way.*

He bends down and photographs the rifle, which is stuck in the bed of the stream.

SECOND FEMALE VOICE over: *To make cinema a revolutionary weapon, you have to think through and with the revolutionary struggle. Think and work out the methods. Class struggle. Armed struggle.*

The INDIAN opens the magazine of the rifle then climbs into the stream, photographing it. Loud music.

TITLE red and black letters and symbols:

1 — THE STRIKE
2 — THE DELEGATE
3 — THE ACTIVE MINORITIES
4 — THE GENERAL ASSEMBLY
5 — REPRESSION

6 — THE ACTIVE STRIKE
7 — THE POLICE STATE
THE ARMED STRUGGLE

Close-up of a drawing showing the mechanism of a bazooka.
SECOND FEMALE VOICE over : *Learn.*

We see a series of diagrams showing a chemical process pinned to a noticeboard. Camera tilts up to show another diagram over a picture of two conical beakers.

SECOND FEMALE VOICE over : *Know how to learn. Read. Calculate. Experiment. Chemistry. Mathematics. Electricity.*

Shot of algebraic symbols chalked on a blackboard . . .

SECOND FEMALE VOICE over : *Read. Plan.*

A circuit diagram from an electrical mechanism . . .

SECOND FEMALE VOICE over : *Learn. Know how to learn. Know how to fight.*

A crudely painted South-east Asian revolutionary poster. Cut to black.

Shot of the front of a sports retailer called OK Sport, cars passing in the street outside.

SECOND FEMALE VOICE over : ' *Good day. Do you have any ping-pong balls? Do you have any skates? Have you got a harpoon? Have you got any tennis racquets? . . . Thank you.' — ' Good-bye, madam.'*

We see a pair of hands fabricating a projectile for a home-made bazooka, tamping down explosives with an empty mineral water bottle.

Shot of a poster advertising a conference in Cuba — July 28 to August 5, 1967.

A hand pulls the trigger of the bazooka — actually a spear gun.

SECOND FEMALE VOICE over : *Warning to militants. Watch out!* Cut to black.

High angle close-up of hands on a sheet of white paper, one hand smearing paint from a tube over the other.

SECOND FEMALE VOICE over : *Warning to militants. Watch out!*

The hand leaves its fingerprints on the piece of paper, then withdraws. Camera zooms down on the paper.

SECOND FEMALE VOICE over : *Warning to militants. Watch out!*

We see a pair of hands opening a brief case, removing a document, closing it again.

SECOND FEMALE VOICE over: *Warning to militants. Watch out!*

Resume on the fingerprints on the piece of paper.

SECOND FEMALE VOICE over: *Warning to militants. Watch out.* Cut to black. *Be prepared to reflect . . .*

Standing on a table are various objects used to make a home-made bomb — photo flash-bulbs, batteries, cable, a timer. The hands of the timer are moving.

SECOND FEMALE VOICE over: *. . . to look ahead, to withdraw. Think. Produce. Simplify. Construct. Wait.* Slow fade out.

Bursts of light and a puff of smoke against a darkened sky accompany a loud explosion on the sound track.

Shot of a ruined factory — the result of the explosion. Cut to black.

Close-up of a small clockwork timer standing in front of a book.

SECOND FEMALE VOICE over: *Reflect. Simplify. Think. Wait.*

The timer reaches the end of its traverse, the arm snaps down, and there is a loud explosion off. The timer jumps on the shelf. The noise of the explosion continues over as we cut back to the ruined factory.

SECOND FEMALE VOICE over: *'Good day, Madam.' . . .* Cut to black. *. . . 'A packet of Chesterfields.' — 'I've only got Gitanes and Gauloises' . . .*

Shot of a pile of Chesterfield cigarettes and half empty packets; several of the cigarettes are painted with red rings, spaced evenly along their length.

SECOND FEMALE VOICE over: *'No. I want Chesterfield.' — 'There's Luckies, Players and Winston' . . .*

We see several books of matches, each with a cigarette tucked behind the match-heads, so that they will ignite all at once when it burns down.

SECOND FEMALE VOICE over: *'No. I want Chesterfield' . . . Wait.*

The book of matches catches fire; there is a loud explosion on the sound track.

The explosion continues as we resume on the shot of the ruined factory. Cut to black.

SECOND FEMALE VOICE over: *Reflect. Simplify.*

Long shot of a Paris street.

SECOND FEMALE VOICE over: *In this street there is a barber's, a baker's, a druggist's, a dairy, a chemist's . . .*

We see containers of chlorate weed-killer, powdered sugar and other items standing on a shelf.

SECOND FEMALE VOICE over: . . . *a novelty shop, a bookshop, etc.*

Close-up of an Expresso coffee pot, a soda siphon and other items.

SECOND FEMALE VOICE over: *You can buy jam, coffee, milk . . .*

Close-up of hands crumbling the ingredients of a home-made explosive into a soup plate with a pair of tweezers.

SECOND FEMALE VOICE over: . . . *sugar, thermos flasks, plates, etc. Think. Produce. Simplify.*

We look down on a street market with stalls on either side.

FIRST FEMALE VOICE over: *It's disgusting. A bomb has been thrown in a supermarket. A lot of people have been injured. What have you got out of it?*

Some people are playing *boule* in an open square, a girl with a moped watching in the foreground.

FIRST FEMALE VOICE over: *It's really unheard of to kidnap Rockefeller's son. What good did that do? The boy hasn't done anything.*

The hands now add the contents of a flash bulb to the mixture in the soup plate.

We see the hands again over the soup plate, inserting an ignition device into the body of a soda siphon.

SECOND FEMALE VOICE over: *Think. Manufacture. Simplify. Reflect. Learn. Learn.*

Close-up of hands applying two bare wires from a coil of cable to a couple of torch batteries strapped together. Sound of an explosion off.

People pass to and fro in front of the *boule* players in the square. The girl in the foreground fiddles with a bag suspended from her moped.

FIRST FEMALE VOICE over: *Fanatics are sent to do the killings, gangsters whose only aim is to kill and destroy, even though no advantage can be gained from it.*

SECOND FEMALE VOICE over: *That's what bourgeois humanitarianism says when the oppressed get the means of grasping the exploiter by the throat. When bourgeois humanitarianism talks about innocent victims, unnecessary violence, what is it hiding? . . .*

Shot of car lamps moving along a road in the darkness.

SECOND FEMALE VOICE over: . . . *The daily reality of bourgeois terror, the reality of the struggle.*

We see a factory entrance in the early morning, dim figures moving to and fro. Cars move past in the foreground.

SECOND FEMALE VOICE over : *Citroën. Javel. Morning shift. The brotherhood of classes in opposition ...*

A closer shot of the same scene. A man is handing out leaflets to workers as they go into the factory. He is joined by another.

SECOND FEMALE VOICE over : *That fraternity which was proclaimed in '89, '71 and '68, written in giant letters on every wall in Paris, all over the walls of the gaols and barracks; that is the real, authentic expression in prose of civil war in its most horrible form, the war between labour and capital. Let us now consider the secondary aspect of the war between labour and capital. But why should we think about that secondary aspect just now? Because the bourgeoisie are now making it their main battlefield. Fine. Think about the secondary aspects of the civil war between labour and capital. Think: primary contradiction and secondary contradiction. Think: the main aspect of the contradiction and the secondary aspect. Fine. Primary contradiction: civil war between labour and capital. Secondary contradiction: division of labour and sex.*

TITLE black and red letters and symbols :

       1 — THE STRIKE
       2 — THE DELEGATE
       3 — THE ACTIVE MINORITIES
       4 — THE GENERAL ASSEMBLY
       5 — REPRESSION
       6 — THE ACTIVE STRIKE
       7 — THE POLICE STATE
       CIVIL VIOLENCE

Seen from a low angle, the GIRL in the pink bustle dress eats from the same plate as the CAVALRYMAN. They talk, overlapping the words of the commentary.

SECOND FEMALE VOICE over : *The secondary contradiction is one that the bourgeoisie tries with all the means in its power to present as the primary one — women's magazines, dogmatic sociology, etc.*

GIRL in Italian : *Wash your hands before eating!*

SECOND FEMALE VOICE over : *Fine. Sex and its division from labour is the secondary contradiction. Now for the first aspect of this secondary contradiction.*

CAVALRYMAN in Italian, turning to camera : *Shitheads! Cocksuckers!*
SECOND FEMALE VOICE over : *The sexual urge is tied to the struggle to gain control of the means of production and to the class struggle. Now for the second aspect of the contradiction. The sexual urge is still almost everywhere the primary property of the bourgeoisie. Think: primary contradiction and secondary contradiction.*
GIRL in Italian : *Don't be rude to the waiter!*
SECOND FEMALE VOICE over : *Think: the primary aspects of the contradiction — primary and secondary; and the secondary aspects of the contradiction — primary and secondary. Think: civil war between labour and capital. Think: the division of labour and sex.*
CAVALRYMAN in Italian : *Screw you!*
SECOND FEMALE VOICE over : *Think: negative and positive. Think: negative and positive. Think: union of opposites. Think: struggle. Think: change. Think: eroticism and plus values. Think.*
GIRL in Italian : *Have some respect for your father who gave you your bread.*
CAVALRYMAN in Italian : *You're full of shit right up to the eyeballs!*
SECOND FEMALE VOICE over : *Think: feelings; value. Think: feelings; value. Think: positive matrimony plus negative adultery equals bourgeois unity. Think: to destroy this unity today is revolutionary for a woman. Which revolution? That of '89 . . . Think about the meaning of this: is the problem of the woman very different from the problem of the peasant farmers?*
GIRL in Italian : *Marriage is sacred and inviolable.*
SECOND FEMALE VOICE over : *Think again about the meaning of this: why does the medium-poor Breton marry? And think: why does a Paris foundry owner marry? Keep thinking about the meaning of this: one day in May '68, unmarried workers of the C.G.T. prevented workers from entering the factory in the morning . . .*
CAVALRYMAN in Italian : *Idiots!*
SECOND FEMALE VOICE over : *. . . Then in the evening they went out to lay their student girlfriends in the Sorbonne and the Odéon. Think of the most horrifying form of fraternity between opposing classes. Think about the civil war between labour and capital. Think of subjectivity in class terms. The end . . . Long pause. Beginning of a prolonged struggle. Cut to black. What is to be done? You've made a film, you've criticized it. You've made mistakes, you corrected some of them. Because of this you know a little more about making images and*

sounds. Perhaps now you know better how this production can be transformed. For whom and against whom? Perhaps you have learned something very simple.

WIAZEMSKY over : *It's right to rebel.*

SECOND FEMALE VOICE over : *Marxism consists of a multiplicity of principles, which in the final analysis can be summed up in a single statement: it's right to rebel.*

A high angle long shot shows the UNION DELEGATE in the distance, walking through the flowery meadow seen earlier.

STUDENT over : *A single statement: it's right to rebel.*

SECOND FEMALE VOICE over : *No, Marxism consists of a multiplicity of principles . . .*

WIAZEMSKY over : *Marxism consists of a multiplicity of principles . . .*

STUDENT over : *. . . which can be summed up in a single statement . . .*

SECOND FEMALE VOICE over : *No. Which, in the last analysis, can be summed up . . .*

Camera moves with the UNION DELEGATE as he comes across the CAVALRYMAN sitting on the ground. He taps him on the shoulder and the CAVALRYMAN gets to his feet holding his rifle. The camera tilts down with the UNION DELEGATE as he comes into the foreground and pulls out his book.

WIAZEMSKY and STUDENT over : *Marxism consists of a multiplicity of principles which, in the last analysis, can be summed up in a single statement: it's right to rebel.*

The UNION DELEGATE reads from his book, looking up towards camera.

UNION DELEGATE reading : *'The policy of peaceful co-existence thus translates into present day terms the problem of maintaining world peace. The transformation resulting from the October Revolution and the continuing development of socialism in many countries has, in this respect, created a totally new situation in the world.'*

As he continues to declaim, camera tilts down over the flowers in the meadow, losing him.

UNION DELEGATE reading off : *'Imperialism has lost nothing of its aggressive nature and events only prove this.'*

Camera pans and tracks to the left until we are looking straight down on the INDIAN and the YOUNG MAN in the bloodstained shirt, lying on the ground; ANNA WIAZEMSKY is close by them, partly hidden by the undergrowth.

UNION DELEGATE reading off: '*The growing power of socialist organizations, coupled with the upsurge of national liberation movements, the struggle of the working classes of capitalist countries and the general development of peace-loving forces, have thus made it possible to avoid a new world war and a nuclear catastrophe.*'

As the UNION DELEGATE continues speaking, the bloodstained YOUNG MAN gets to his feet and scrambles up a bank towards camera. WIAZEMSKY starts to follow him.

UNION DELEGATE reading off: '*The policy of peaceful co-existence is a method for regulating . . .*'

Camera tilts up with the YOUNG MAN as he tries to scramble up the bank, but keeps falling back. The UNION DELEGATE reappears in the background.

YOUNG MAN in Italian: *Help me!*

UNION DELEGATE reading: '. . . *is a method for regulating relations between states.*'

The UNION DELEGATE lets down the butt of the CAVALRYMAN's rifle and hauls the YOUNG MAN up the bank. The latter jumps up, grabs the rifle, and points it at the UNION DELEGATE, who throws his arms in the air. As the commentary continues, the YOUNG MAN lets down the rifle and helps first WIAZEMSKY and then the INDIAN up the bank. Camera tilts up as they run away across the meadow, into the distance.

SECOND FEMALE VOICE over: *To dare to rebel — for us, this means fighting here and now on two fronts. To dare to rebel — for you, this means fighting here and now on two fronts* . . . Cut to black . . . *Fighting against the eternal lies of the bourgeoisie.*

Rapid close-up of the GIRL being made up, as we saw her at the beginning of the film. An assistant is holding up a colour chart in front of her face. Cut to black.

SECOND FEMALE VOICE over: *The modernization of our economy is a vital task, and if we fail, we are left with a limited independence and stagnation* . . .

Rapid shot of the red-washed walls of the building seen at the beginning of the film. The CAVALRYMAN passes up the slope in the foreground, carrying his rifle. Cut to black.

SECOND FEMALE VOICE over: . . . *which will automatically lead to rebellion. Only a flourishing and efficient economy will enable us* . . .

Rapid high angle shot of the GIRL in the pink bustle dress, shooting something on the ground with her cine-camera. Cut to black.

SECOND FEMALE VOICE over : *. . . to strengthen the foundations under us and give us real solidarity.*

Rapid shot of the UNION DELEGATE and the CAVALRYMAN as seen earlier, discussing the fate of the INDIAN. Cut to black.

SECOND FEMALE VOICE over : *But if we are to succeed in this difficult enterprise, we must drastically change our habitual ways of acting and thinking. It is everyone's duty to help to bring about this change.*

Shot of the GIRL having her eyes made up, as seen earlier. Her hair is clipped back and she is wearing a red sweater.

SECOND FEMALE VOICE over : *In this technological society, with its complex mechanisms which are so difficult to understand . . .* Cut to black *. . . participation is the right way to involve people in recognizing . . .*

We return to the CAVALRYMAN and the GIRL in the pink bustle dress eating from the same plate. Cut to black.

SECOND FEMALE VOICE over : *. . . that they are masters of their own destiny.*

CHORUS OF SHOUTS off : *Death to the bourgeoisie!*

There is loud triumphant singing as WIAZEMSKY, followed by the YOUNG MAN, frogmarches the UNION DELEGATE up a road towards us. The INDIAN moves across to the left carrying a rifle. They place the DELEGATE with his back to them at the side of the road, then camera pans across as they join a firing squad on the opposite side. They all take aim.

SECOND FEMALE VOICE over : *To dare to rebel — for us, this means fighting here and now on two fronts, against the bourgeoisie and its ally, revisionism.*

TITLE black and red letters :

THERE ARE IN THE WORLD TODAY TWO
WINDS — THE EAST WIND AND THE WEST
WIND. THE EAST WIND ACTUALLY PRE-
VAILS OVER THE WEST WIND. THE RE-
VOLUTIONARY FORCES HAVE ACHIEVED
AN OVERWHELMING SUPERIORITY OVER
THE IMPERIALIST FORCES.

Cut to black.